Praise for *A Poetics of Orthodoxy*

"We need a book like this for poetry and Christianity in the twenty-first century."
—Mark Jarman

"Myers provides us more tools for cultivating a poetic imagination, so we may better hear the voice of God."
—Jessica Hooten Wilson

"*A Poetics of Orthodoxy* movingly and soundly puts beauty in its rightful place: at the heart of God and at the center of human perception."
—Karen Swallow Prior

"Benjamin Myers shows just why it is that Christians will become better Christians by understanding poetry and beauty, and why poets will become better poets by undertaking the adventure of Christian orthodoxy.... Myers builds from the ground up to show us a better way to be human in a sadly 'excarnated' world."
—James Matthew Wilson

Praise for Benjamin P. Myers

"Myers has a great gift for narrative, and these poems ring with honesty and tenderness, finding a real poignancy in moments from the past. *The Family Book of Martyrs* reminds the reader of the sacredness available in the give-and-take of family life, a holiness of routine decisions and daily sacrifices."
—*Psaltery and Lyre*

"Benjamin Myers brings the full array of his powers to this gorgeous collection: his elegance and erudition; his gifts as a storyteller; his wise, unsentimental, tender heart. Through the voices of people who lived it, [in *Black Sunday*] Myers bears witness to some of the most iconic scenes of the Dust Bowl."
—Rilla Askew

"Benjamin Myers delights and surprises us by his startling imagery and technical skill, but even more by a rueful awareness of the swiftness of time, and the wonder of the ordinary events that fill it."
—Lynne Sharon Schwartz

"[In *Elegy for Trains*,] Myers comes across as—among other good things—the Woody Guthrie-meets-Walt Whitman of today's Oklahoma. And he does it with the heart of a native and erudition of a scholar."
—Nathan Brown

AMBIGUITY & BELONGING

Fort Smith, Arkansas

AMBIGUITY & BELONGING

ESSAYS ON PLACE, EDUCATION, & POETRY

BENJAMIN P. MYERS

Ambiguity and Belonging:
Essays on Place, Education, and Poetry

Cover design by Corey Lee Fuller

Edited by Casie Dodd

Belle Point Press, LLC
Fort Smith, Arkansas
bellepointpress.com
editor@bellepointpress.com

Find Belle Point Press
on Facebook, Substack,
and Instagram (@bellepointpress)

Printed in the United States of America

28 27 26 25 24   1 2 3 4 5

Library of Congress Control Number: 2024949490

ISBN: 978-1-960215-26-0

AMB / BPP39

Contents

Foreword

THESE ESSAYS, covering a range of topics over a long span of time, are meant to be no more unified and coherent than the personality of their author. Thus their only organizing principle is the scope of my preoccupations. These are the things I think about.

I don't suppose myself to be particularly wise, which raises the question of why you would want to spend your time reading my thoughts. I offer them merely in the spirit of conversation. I don't believe much in my own wisdom or insight, but conversation—*that* I believe in. These essays are simply my side of the discussion we would have if you were to visit me sometime here at my home and we were to sit down on the porch for a good while and talk things through. I'm certain I would learn much and gain much perspective from your end of the conversation, and I can only hope that the same would be true a little for you as I talk.

I rarely spend time with other people without leaving with the feeling that I have talked too much, listened too little. So I can only beg your pardon for the argumentative tone I take at times in these essays. I get swept up in the flow of talk. I don't mean to be rude. Take away with you from this conversation what you are inclined to take, and let the rest drift off on the wind. There is lots of good talk to be had with both the living and dead. Take the conversation I offer here only for what it is worth. I'm grateful to spend a little time with you.

Chandler, OK
October, 2023

Part I

Ambiguity and Belonging in Oklahoma

IT IS A STRANGE THING to firmly belong to a land that only tentatively and ambiguously belongs to you. It is a strange thing to be deeply rooted in the place your wandering ancestors happened to land a few generations ago. It is a strange thing to feel intimately bound to a piece of earth you no longer depend upon to sustain you. It is a strange thing to be an Oklahoman.

Like many Southerners, I can trace a great portion of my roots to the Scots-Irish immigrants who spread out from Pennsylvania, down through Appalachia, and west into Oklahoma and Texas. Thus, I come from a somewhat rootless people. Though they would have often been described as "settlers," they were a people known more for their movement than for their settlement: from Scotland to Ireland; from Ireland to America; from the North to the South; from the South to the West. Their story is told well in Jim Webb's book *Born Fighting*. They were Protestant dissenters looking for a place to worship as they saw fit. Then they were the poor and fiercely independent looking for a place where they could live free. They were a strong and often skilled group of people, but they were also a people habitually "up against it" and looking for a place to scrap together a better life.

This search for something better led my maternal forebears into Oklahoma sometime in the late nineteenth century, where they settled in the hills just west of the Arkansas border, part of a small western outpost of Appalachia. Both of my maternal grandparents were born there, and I have family ties there still. Following the oil fields, however, eventually brought my grandparents to central Oklahoma, where my mother graduated from high school, I graduated from high school, and—just this past May—my oldest daughter also graduated from high school. Religion, opportunity, and oil brought me to this place. A lifetime spent here has bound me to it.

Most of Oklahoma can still be described as rural. None of my grandparents were full-time farmers in adulthood, but they still carried the memories, habits, and practices of a people living by the land. They were rural people. They raised cattle and grew vegetables to supplement the income earned from other work. They lived through the Great Depression in Oklahoma, so they knew how to survive. Remarkably, while so many packed up and continued the great Scots-Irish migration west, my grandparents did not, likely because none of them were living in the panhandle where the dust was the worst. Or perhaps something in their wandering DNA finally gave out, and it just seemed better to stay for once. For whatever reason, they finally stuck. And now I am stuck too. Or rather, I'm choosing to stick.

I live in the town in which I grew up, the town I have always lived in with the exception of the few years I spent on higher education elsewhere. So to put that numerically, I have lived in Chandler, Oklahoma, for thirty-six of my forty-eight years: the first eighteen years and the last eighteen years so far. I have done so because I have chosen to do so. My wife and I have made this choice together, to return to and spend the rest of our lives in the town in which we grew up, met, and fell in love. This choice has not been without practical considerations. It is useful to have family nearby to provide childcare from time to time, and it is reassuring to have a general support network should we need it. Also, it is nice to live in a place with a reasonable cost of living, which has afforded us a more comfortable lifestyle and a greater amount of security than we would likely have most other places. The bulk of our decision, however, has not been practical but rather more spiritual in nature. In short, we want to belong to a place. We want to live a life together in acknowledgement that our life is not of our own making. And, since this is the place with a prior claim to us both, this is the place we have stuck.

Yet while Oklahoma's claim on me is strong, I know that, from one way of looking at it, my claim on Oklahoma is substantially weaker. The poor Scots-Irish settlers who flooded into Oklahoma before and after it was officially opened may not have been the ones calling the shots in their nation's treatment of its native population, but they were the seemingly unstoppable force that swept into the Southern Plains and pushed aside the previous inhabitants as irresistibly as their own ancient relatives were swept aside by the Germanic waves that crashed into the British isles in the early Middle Ages. No more than three or four generations before me, this land was taken from one people and appropriated by another people. The later people, the takers, were my people.

The place where I live was opened to white settlement in a second land run shortly after the famous Oklahoma Land Run of 1891, apparently because the survey was not finished in time for the big run. When I was a child, this land run was commemorated yearly by school children dressed as pioneers. I vividly remember taking my turn as an original settler of the Chandler area. Like most of the boys in my class, I somewhat anachronistically insisted on dressing more like a movie cowboy than a pioneer. Fortunately, small boys in Oklahoma are accustomed to running in stiff, knobby-heeled cowboy boots. They gave us plastic tent stakes and sent us running across an empty field adjacent to the city park so that we could stake out a little claim for ourselves. We then celebrated with sack lunches and games. Years later, my own children went through this yearly ritual, and, as far as I know, Chandler kids are still running for little plots of Oklahoma earth today.

The story of Oklahoma settlement is, of course, much more complex and complicated than any elementary school field day can capture, but I believe the impulse to remember, even to reenact, is correct. Correct too are the various efforts of the tribes that have occupied and still occupy this land to remember their story. The Sac and Fox and Iowa tribes were relocated only a few decades before the land run to the former Osage hunting ground that would eventually become Lincoln County, Oklahoma. The new white settlement did not straightfor-wardly replace the recent tribal settlement but, rather, overlaid it. The result is layers of culture, a far more complicated and interesting story than the dominant myth of simple replacement. When urban dwellers elsewhere dismiss Oklahoma as "lacking diversity," I like to point out that I drive through several sovereign territories on my way to work. To whom does the land belong? Are our field-day commemorations really claims of ultimate ownership, a way of marking the land "ours"? Or are they the fragmented pieces of a whole picture that is hard to see from where any of us stand, which is on the land in question itself?

It is hard to say who this land belongs to, but I know without a doubt that I belonged to it from my earliest youth. I was raised just south of town, on a defunct dairy farm surrounded by miles of pasture and scrubby woods. I can barely remember a time before I was allowed to roam over that countryside freely. As long as we didn't interfere with the cattle, the ranchers who lived around us didn't mind if my sisters and I fished in their ponds and played in their woods. From eight years old on, I was adept at moving over, under, or through a barbwire fence. I knew which of the houses scattered along the dirt roads had dogs that should not be approached. I know where the clumps of scrub oak and invasive eastern cedar would give out into open field, where erosion created gullies suitable for trench warfare, and where little creeks populated with crawdads lazily slumped into swampish ponds thick with tadpoles and bullfrogs. I knew when the hay was cut, baled, and hauled under the relentless heat of the sun. I came to know the rhythms of the year in this particular place. I became accustomed to seeing the sky from here.

Soon I added to this connection to the countryside a close coexistence with the town itself. Many of the businesses I frequent today are places I accompanied my parents or grandparents to when I was a child. Other shops have been started by people I have known for years and perhaps even grown up with. Not that our streets haven't changed. Businesses have, of course, come and gone, but I feel all the more bound to this place by the experience of the change, by being part of a living community neither fossilized nor completely discontinuous with the past. The neighborhoods around town both are and are not the same as in my boyhood. Some houses are unchanged; others are gone. Some houses have fallen into dilapidation; others have been renovated. Trees have grown larger, been cut down, or been trimmed back. All of this has happened mostly before my eyes.

I don't have a much better reason than that for being here. I'm a professor and a writer, work that could be done just about anywhere, perhaps with greater ease than it can be done among my admittedly often anti-intellectual rural brethren. My wife's family is still mostly in the area, which is no doubt a very good reason for us to be here, but all of my immediate family, and most of my relatives, have passed away or moved away. Maybe, in part, I'm here as a last foothold for my clan. Or maybe I'm just here for sentimental reasons. But I think it is more than that. I think I am here because a decision to stick has to be made at some point, and because, no matter how bloody and unjust the history of a place may be, there is no sense in simply running from the past. Even in America someone has to answer the call to dwell in the complexity of history.

It might seem strange to love a place merely for long association with it, but most of our loves are formed that way. That this long association begins in accident, both historical and familial, is no mark against it. Most of our meaningful connections are not of our own making. We are given to a place through the apparent accidents of birth, though with faith we may sense the hand of providence behind it all.

In "The Gift Outright," Robert Frost succinctly sums up early American experience by noting that "the land was ours before we were the land's." I suspect such was the case for much longer among the restless Scots-Irish and further west than Frost's beloved New England. But it is important to note that the "gift" in the title is not the land. The gift is ourselves. Frost presents this gift of self to place as a deliberate act: "Such as we were we gave ourselves outright." Living with the ambiguities and contradictions, I deliberately make this gift of myself, such as I am, in hopes that it will also be a gift of my children and for my children. Although I will not attempt to constrain them, I hope my children and their children will accept the gift and accept being given, by the chances of their births, to this place. To sustain the sort of continuity that sustains the sense of responsibility to build, to pass on, and to do right before the silent witness of our ancestors and our descendants requires a staying in place. Rootlessness and the constant search for new opportunity are part of the American story, but if starting over is the only story, we lose more than a physical inheritance. We lose the spiritual, moral, and cultural inheritance that gives our lives meaningful shape and purpose. I believe we see the fruits of rootlessness in the cultural disintegration evident in our popular culture, politics, and academic discourse. For the common good and for their own good, I pray that my people will finally stick.

Hunting Berryman's Ghost in Oklahoma

WHEN I WAS A KID, my parents sometimes took me Oklahoma ghost hunting. They would load my sisters and me into the car and drive to some reputedly haunted location. I remember vividly our visit to a haunted hanging tree in the Cimarron valley, its broad reach of branches seemingly still bowed by the weight of the dead. The explanation for these strange family outings is that my parents were writers, and I suppose they were hunting ghost stories more than actual ghosts. Like their love of stories and their love of words, my parents' hobby hunting ghosts must have rubbed off on me, because I find myself hunting my own Oklahoma spirit: the ghost of the great American poet John Berryman.

In the penultimate poem of the published version of Berryman's *Dream Songs*, Henry, the persona adopted by the poet, stands at his father's grave where the "marker slants, flowerless" and admits that "often, often before / I've made this awful pilgrimage." Of course, *The Dream Songs* is a book of poems obsessed with the suicide of the poet's father, so the pilgrimage in question may be entirely metaphorical. Nevertheless, it makes me wonder how often, if ever, Berryman did in fact return to visit his father's grave, where the body lies, as Berryman says in Dream Song #143 "stashed in Oklahoma," or as he says in #292, "ruined in a grave in Oklahoma." While there are in his *Dream Songs* few mentions of the state in which Berryman was born, what reference he does make to Oklahoma makes it clear he associates the place with his lost father, and in Berryman's poems, the lost father is everywhere central.

John Berryman was born in McAlester in October of 1914.[1] His father, John Allyn Smith (the poet takes the name Berryman from the man his mother married after Smith's suicide), was a banker from Minnesota. His mother was a schoolteacher and met his father while teaching in Sasakwa, Oklahoma—a tiny town in Seminole County, near McAlester, remembered today primarily as the site of the Green Corn Rebellion in 1917. Berryman's family was, by then, living in nearby Lamar. Of course, being just three at the time, it is extremely doubtful that the poet had any memory of the Oklahoma radicals' planned protest against the draft or of their confrontation with local citizens, during which three people were killed.

The Smith family moved around the southern part of the state quite a bit during Berryman's early years. After the 1916 move to Lamar, two years later they moved again, to Wagoner, where Berryman's younger brother was born, and then in 1921 they settled in Anadarko. Like many Oklahomans and Texans at the time, they were following the oil money, as Berryman's father took a job as a loan officer at First State Bank. The young poet-to-be attended school in Anadarko and was an altar boy at a local Catholic church. Eventually his father left the banking business and became assistant game and fish warden for the State of Oklahoma. Despite this seeming success, however, in 1925 young John's parents left for Florida to get in on the land boom. John and his brother were left behind to board at St. Joseph's Academy in Chickasha, Oklahoma, but, miserable at the school, they were retrieved by their mother before the end of the year and taken

---

1. For the basic facts, I have relied on Paul Mariani's superb biography of Berryman: *Dream Song: The Life of John Berryman* (William Morrow and Company, 1990).

to Florida. Thus, the poet's time in Oklahoma ended when he was only eleven, but many of the factors that would influence him as an artist were already in play, including the smoldering disintegration of his parents' marriage—including the infidelities and deceptions that would contribute to his father's suicide in Florida the following year.

From this beginning, Berryman became one of the most significant American poets of the mid-twentieth century. His masterpiece, the 385-poem sequence known as *The Dream Songs*, won him both a Pulitzer Prize and a National Book Award. The strangely obscure, purposefully illogical nature of his writing, along with his intensely personal subject matter, made him—along with poets like Robert Lowell, Sylvia Plath, and Allen Ginsberg—part of the transition from the modernism of the first half of the twentieth century to the postmodernism of its second half.

Vaguely aware of his reputation for being a "difficult" poet, I first read Berryman hesitantly and only because he was born in Oklahoma (how I knew that I don't recall). His wit, imagination, linguistic acrobatics, and emotional honesty soon won me over, and I quickly learned to go along for the ride in a wild Berryman poem, not trying to arrive at a "meaning" for the poem that could be paraphrased but, rather, absorbing the mood suggested by the images and allusions. A Berryman poem is often puzzling, but it is generally best to treat it not as a puzzle but as an experience. As he says himself, "These Songs are not meant to be understood, you understand. / They are only meant to terrify & comfort." Soon, I was gobbling up Dream Songs like candy—disturbing, heartbreaking, hilarious candy. But I continued to wonder how this place where he was born, and where he lived such formative years, marked his soul and thus his poetry.

Berryman's relationship with Oklahoma matters to me for several reasons. I want to be able to claim him, alongside Ralph Ellison and N. Scott Momaday, as a great literary figure who belongs to

Oklahoma. It's about Okie pride. Also, as a poet, a professor, and a reader, I want to understand his work better, to get to something mysterious at its root. But also, and maybe primarily, I just want to feel closer to a poet whose work has come to matter greatly to me, whose work has, indeed, both terrified and comforted me. I want to share this place with a writer who has touched me deeply.

Both of the standard biographies of Berryman, while excellent, move fairly quickly past his early days in Oklahoma, presumably because there is little source material to work from on that time between the poet's birth in October of 1914 and the family's departure for Florida in 1925. Perhaps, also, Berryman's biographers are understandably in a hurry to get to the 1926 suicide of the poet's father, as that is the event that so dramatically runs throughout Berryman's greatest work. Yet the first eleven years of one's life are surely important. "The Child is father of the Man," Wordsworth famously said, and the young Berryman must have been affected, as I was, by spending his formative years in rural Oklahoma.

As I sit at my desk writing, I look out the window at the large sycamore across the street, a tree much like the large sycamore that grew in front of the house where I grew up, and I think of Dream Song #1, specifically of the poignant lines toward the end: "Once in a sycamore I was glad / all at the top, and I sang." This first poem in Berryman's magnum opus is a version of *Paradise Lost*. "All the world like a woolen lover / once did seem on Henry's side. / Then came a departure," Berryman writes in the voice of his alter-ego. The image of singing in a sycamore is an image of boyish freedom and, as Berryman's best biographer, the poet Paul Mariani, points out, gestures toward the poet's childhood in rural Oklahoma. So in the very first poem of Berryman's masterpiece, Oklahoma is associated with the lost paradise of childhood innocence. This symbolic connection between Oklahoma and a paradise lost is evoked again in

Dream Song #195, where Berryman laments, "Oklahoma, sore / from my great loss leaves me." For Berryman, Oklahoma seems to be, to borrow a title from his good friend Randall Jarrell, "The Lost World." This association helps us make sense of the first poem's second-to-last line, which tells us that "Hard on the land wears the strong sea." The image is perhaps Berryman's cryptic way of remembering the move from the safe interior of the country to seaside Florida, where things went terribly wrong for the family.

Several times in *The Dream Songs* Berryman offers idyllic, almost Edenic, memories of life in Oklahoma. In #11 he recalls skating up and down in front of the house of a childhood crush. Speaking in the third person he describes his pining younger self as "wishing he could, sir, die," an expression of childhood passion which seems almost whimsical when contrasted with the more pronounced death wish that runs through so much of the other poems in the volume. In #167, he comically contrasts the poor postal service in his current city with "the town in Okie-land when I was young— / three and four deliveries a day!" I'm no expert on the history of the postal service, but I suspect this fantastic service is embellished by Berryman's imagination. In #241, he recalls watching his father march with his National Guard unit on a rainy hillside in Oklahoma, which he describes as "a fraction of sun & guns / 'way 'way ago," a kind of boy's paradise. In all three of these poems, Oklahoma is the faraway place, the unrecoverable golden world before the fall. I find no mention in the biographies or in Berryman's published letters of a return to Oklahoma for so much as a visit. Is it possible he thought it impossible to come back here?

Wanting to see what Berryman's Oklahoma looked like, I decide to drive down to Anadarko, an Oklahoma town just a few hours south of my own, one summer morning after seeing my wife and children off for their day. I chose Anadarko, rather than McAlester, because I want to see the Oklahoma that imprinted Berryman's soul, the town in which he was a boy being far more important to his development than the accident of where he spent his earliest days. I don't want to diminish McAlester's claim to the great writer—his birthplace matters—but Anadarko would be what Berryman remembered best as Oklahoma.

I drive down past Oklahoma City on I-44 and then take Highway 62 from Chickasha to Anadarko. The land heading into Anadarko is very typically Oklahoma, not so much flat as rolling but still wide, wide open under endless domed blue sky. Round bales and pump-jacks are scattered across the yellowed fields along the highway, with an occasional silo reaching into sky. There is smoke in the distance, perhaps from a controlled burn. I feel hopeful about encountering a ghost.

Mariani's biography, which begins with the conjuring of Berryman's ghost and which may have given me the idea for this hunt, gives the Berrymans' address in Anadarko, and I find the street immediately. Before I left, my wife asked why I didn't just check Google Maps to see if the house (described by Mariani as a white, five-room home) is still there. I suppose I'm on a pilgrimage, and every pilgrimage should involve some mystery and some risk. I suppose, too, that I am equally interested in seeing what remains of Berryman's life in Oklahoma and in seeing what kinds of erasure have occurred, what the "ruins of time" have done to the markers of his life here. After all, ghosts are more likely to haunt ruins than they are to haunt museums.

The house that matches the number fits the description well. It's a small bungalow that could have easily been built before the Berrymans' arrival. It may be a little larger, but driving around, I see that the back portion is an obvious addition. I can't believe my luck. I think about going to the door and asking the owners if they are aware of their illustrious predecessor in occupancy. There is, however, a low wire fence around the entire property and a number of "Beware of

Dog" signs, so I decide that they are perhaps not interested in literary visitors. Besides, the lack of any vehicle outside the home suggests that no one is home. I content myself with sitting parked, stalker-like, on the street and taking pictures on my phone. It is while glancing around for patrolmen or neighborhood watch that I notice the fine print on the street sign: "E. Kentucky." I double check Mariani's book. The Berrymans lived on W. Kentucky. I am on the wrong side of town, joyfully communing with a ghost unlikely to haunt here. Although I'm embarrassed, I can't help thinking that Berryman, whose life often seemed like one long series of comic/tragic mishaps, would enjoy my error. His poetic technique suggests he enjoys being evasive.

I follow Kentucky to the other side of town, which is easy to do despite a short detour around the feed store and farm center that takes up several blocks. When I reach the appropriate block on the west side, I find few houses, all on the wrong side of the street. The entire block on the Berrymans' side of the street is occupied by the Caddo Baptist Association and a crisis pregnancy center. The Berryman home is gone. Judging from the architecture, I'd guess it was demolished sometime around midcentury to make room for the large church that is now the Baptist Association and pregnancy center.

The surrounding neighborhood, however, is much as I pictured it. Many of the original homes remain, any number of which could have belonged to Berryman's childhood playmates. I wonder which house might be the one little John skated back and forth in front of hoping to catch sight of pretty Charlotte and "wishing he could, sir, die." I wonder which one might have belonged to the Callahan family, whose son F.J. impressed Berryman by being the first person he knew to die—a death, as he recounts it in Dream Song #129, which took place by a cottonwood tree and made the boy permanently "a part of Henry's history."

The block seems cut short by a four-lane street, another development that no doubt helped to erase Berryman's history in Anadarko. I get back into my car and drive across the four-lane. Circling the block, I spot a large, low-limbed sycamore, very suitable for climbing. "Once in a sycamore I was glad / all at the top, and I sang." It is a very small, very uncertain victory, but I gladly take it.

Next, I go looking for the site of the Holy Family Catholic Church, where young John was confirmed and served as an altar boy under a priest he remembered fondly all his life, a memory Mariani connects to Berryman's return to the Catholic faith toward the end of his life. This time, I'm not expecting to find the church, as I've already read online about how the congregation relocated and renamed years ago, leaving the church to be torn down and replaced by an apartment complex. I drive slowly by the apartments. I wonder if anyone living there has read Berryman. Do they know they are walking on ground that was once hallowed by worship and by the presence of future literary greatness? Is there a bookcase here with *The Dream Songs* displayed?

I've come to Anadarko looking for a ghost, and after a morning of driving around and walking shady sidewalks, I feel like that ghost has remained just outside my perceptual grasp, like Berryman's own elusive, allusive, and disorienting poems. I haven't understood, but I have been comforted. But can I read *The Dream Songs* better for having been here? I think I can, if only in that I can more perfectly picture the sidewalks, the trees, the whole setting of those poems that touch on his life in Oklahoma.

It's almost 1:00 now, and I am hungry. On the way out of town, I stop at a renovated soda fountain and sandwich shop on old Main Street Anadarko. I'm still just a few blocks from Berryman's house and church. Reading the framed history of the building, I see that it was begun in 1901 as Dinkler Drug and operated for much of the twentieth century. It is easy to imagine young Berryman sent here to pick up prescriptions for his high-strung mother. It is easy to imagine him stopping in for a soda with Charlotte or F.J. or any of his friends. I have no evidence that he ever did so, but I enjoy imagining a young man—before the move and his father's suicide, before the struggle and the fame and the devastating drinking—taking a few moments of simple enjoyment here. When I return to my car, Berryman's face looks bemused on the cover of Mariani's biography, which I have left in the passenger seat.

If Berryman's ghost haunts anywhere, one would expect to find him lingering around the bridge in Minneapolis from which, following his father's example, he jumped to his death. But I wonder if his spirit doesn't also return to the green, low hills around McAlester, to the wind-swept plains of Anadarko. Does John Berryman haunt Oklahoma, as Oklahoma seemed to haunt him? All I can say is that his spirit haunts me and eludes me. It keeps me reading. It keeps me hunting.

Leviathan and the Covenant of
Local Commerce

THE MAIN STREET of Chandler, my hometown, runs from sky to sky atop a rolling hill in the pasture-land of central Oklahoma. The buildings shouldered up along its narrow strip date mostly from the turn of the last century, and their brownstone and red brick bear the scars of a hundred years of wind, dust, and commerce. They've withstood drought and depression. They've withstood the drain of two world wars. They've withstood a changing world, from the sixties to the new millennium. Then came the Super Walmart.

For years we had made do with a regular Walmart, squatting like a fat chicken just on the edge of town and maiming our main street commerce without managing to completely kill it. I remember well the big box's arrival, sometime back in the eighties of my childhood, because one of the casualties was my favorite variety store. "Wacker's" was one of the last five-and-dimes and a wonderland of basic necessities and unusual treats. My sisters and I would hunt up all the change we could find around the house and head across the bridge, over the tracks (the wrong side of which we lived on), and up to Main Street to return an hour later with a cherry slush and a handful of little rubber men with parachutes. Whacker's provided toothpaste and deodorant, paintbrushes and plastic tarps, but the

Walmart quickly took Whacker's out, along with a long-standing department store next door. We also lost a neighborhood grocery store and the Otasco (Oklahoma Tire and Supply), where we bought bicycles, bicycle pumps, and various tools. Our main street, on the whole however, managed to survive better than most. We kept a drugstore, a clothing store, a flower shop, a hardware store, and a couple of restaurants. Then, like a virus made stronger by the efforts to kill it, came the "Super"—drug-resistant—version of Walmart, making it even more urgent to save our main street.

Main Street is worth saving because a town needs a heart in order to have a soul. Small towns across the country are being stripped of their identity, processed like factory beef into an endless line of McTowns stretching from one coast to the other: a super store just outside town, a line of strip mall parasites stringing out around it, and an endless swirl of "subdivisions" providing "country living" on half-acre plots ever more distant from a decaying downtown. This economic entropy is rapidly erasing America, making it nearly impossible at times to really be anywhere very specific at all. Some people may find this uniformity comforting, but I don't think that is a healthy kind of comfort.

A healthy downtown gives definition and particularity to a community. Its businesses provide a picture of who we are. In Chandler, the hardware store testifies to our self-reliance. Until recently, the local bank—the loans of which have kept our businesses afloat, our farms productive, and our roofs over our heads—testified to our interdependence, though it too has now been replaced by a chain. The furniture store speaks of our commitment to homemaking and hospitality. These are the stores where we've purchased our work boots, our suits and ties, our modest but sturdy bedroom furniture. These stores are owned and operated by our neighbors and our friends, and to live in a community is to enter an economic covenant with its other members. By virtue just of planting ourselves here, we enter into a covenant of mutual support, economic and otherwise. It is unconscionable to betray that covenant for a cheap thrill on the edge of town. As long as they are honest and keep their eye not just on profit but also on the common good, then we owe our neighbors our commerce. Walmart's ability to buy cheap goods in vast quantities and undercut small businesses does not change that. Keeping our towns healthy is worth spending a few dollars more on our jeans and our coffee cups.

A healthy downtown tells us who we've been. An abandoned downtown can, of course, also be a reminder of the past, but it's the difference between a living monument and an archive. A vibrant main street brings us daily into the same world in which our mothers and fathers lived. It means something to buy a wrench from the daughter of the man your father bought his wrenches from. A living main street reminds us that there was a time before now and that, in T.S. Eliot's memorable phrase, "Time past is time present." We are connected to the people of the past; we gain strength from their strength, humility from their weakness. To go about our business in the buildings they have built is a powerful reminder of that connection. Civilized people don't just abandon their past.

When a people do abandon their past, they inevitably invite monsters into the present. Witness the endless hordes of obviously predatory businesses that are moving into empty downtowns across America. Many American downtowns are now dominated by businesses that see a widespread loss of hope as a great opportunity for profit: the discount liquor stores, the pawn shops, the rapidly multiplying marijuana operations, and—perhaps worst of all—the "loan companies." These loan businesses are vultures on the corpse of local economy. The so-called "payday loans" they offer are little more than racketeering, with interest rates hundreds of times that of a standard loan. These companies may offer loans to people who couldn't get them otherwise, but the borrowers are inevitably left in far worse shape when the loan is due. A healthy downtown moves goods and services for the benefit of all, an economy in the truest sense of the word. "Payday loans" and their ilk feed like a cancer until the community dies. When a Walmart draws business out of downtown, it produces the perfect conditions for that cancer to thrive.

That the advent of a big-box store can bring such deterioration is more than mere conjecture. Kenneth Stone, professor of economics at Iowa State, has spent years studying the effects of big retail on local businesses. By observing a wide variety of local retailers over long periods of time, he has demonstrated that the adverse effects of the Walmart phenomenon are undeniable. In one study, Stone proved that retailers in small towns in Iowa—towns, like my hometown, with populations under five thousand—have lost nearly half of their retail trade due to the presence of Walmart stores.[1] In a study of Walmart's impact in Mississippi, Stone found a "zero-sum game" effect, meaning that Walmart's gain is inevitably someone else's loss.[2] Stacy Mitchell, a senior researcher with the Institute for Local Self-Reliance, enumerates the losses in individual categories, explaining that, "[s]ince 1990, the U.S. has lost some 11,000 pharmacies, 5,000 hardware stores, 2,000 bookstores, and an untold number of grocers, clothing stores, and other independent retailers."[3] What

---

1. Kenneth E. Stone, "Impact of the Wal-Mart Phenomenon on Rural Communities" in *Increasing Understanding of Public Problems and Policies* (The Farm Foundation, 1997), 16.
2. Kenneth E. Stone, Georgeanne Artz, and Albert Myles, "The Economic Impact of Wal-Mart Supercenters on Existing Businesses in Mississippi" (Mississippi State University Extension Services, 2003), 25.
3. Stacy Mitchell, "Small Businesses and Wal-Mart," *Social Policy* 36 (2005): 13. See also www.hometownadvantage.org.

these scholars describe is the rapid dissolution of the character of our hometowns, the surrender of our local culture, and the loss of our economic independence.

What to do, then, other than hunker down and wait for the discount darkness to descend? Obviously we can resist the incursion of the big stores, organizing community meetings and, if necessary, protests. Some communities have successfully held off big-box incursion through sheer grassroots effort. For most small-town citizens, however, Super Walmart is no more to be resisted than a hurricane. I recall no meetings, no community discussion. We were simply told that Walmart is coming, and by the time we were told, it was a foregone conclusion. When the cancer is diagnosed at this late stage, it is easy to feel helpless. If our first thought is to refuse shopping at the super store, our second thought is often on the futility of such "drop in the bucket" gestures. Is the Walmart Supercenter, in its economic might, really going to notice if I go elsewhere for milk and motor oil?

Of course, we could organize a broader boycott. Local business advocates in Austin have organized large-scale chain-store dropouts on certain days. Still, such boycotts most likely exercise power more through symbolism than through real economic impact, enlightening a few more people but really not doing much to discourage the big box store itself. Anyway, I doubt such a wide-scale action could be organized in a rural community where far fewer citizens are inclined to activism and where the simple novelty of a new store can be an overwhelming temptation, not to mention the draw of cheaper, if less durable, goods.

So I, along with a few like-minded friends, will almost certainly be no more able to drive the Walmart away than we were to keep it from arriving in the first place. All I can do, then, is strive to keep my

covenant with my local merchants and encourage others to do the
same. A large, impersonal box store and its online analogs threaten
to remove the "You and I" element from economic exchange. I can
resist that particular form of cultural decline by doing business with
people I know. In the end, Walmart will neither know nor care that
I am shopping elsewhere, but you and I will. And perhaps if we each
make an effort to draw others in our community into that covenant,
supporting local business in word and in dollar, our main street can
hold on for another twenty years. This may seem little more than a
thin hope shored against the tide of modern consumer culture, but
hope—along with hard work, dust, and brick—is the stuff from
which we built our main street.

My family will continue to make as much use of main-street
businesses as we can, and we will work to wean ourselves off of
the online Leviathans as well. As of now, we still have a thriving
main street within short walking distance from our home. There
is a drugstore, a furniture store, a hardware store, a florist, and a
clothing store that all not only survive but seem to thrive. The local
feed and seed has built a new, impressive building and continues to
serve as a community hub. There is also still a movie theater—the
old kind with a single screen—on our main street, where I can take
my family to a movie and buy snacks without needing to take out a
loan to do so. While some restaurants have gone, others have come
along to replace them, including a wonderful pizza place. A com-
munity-minded local phone company has put in a coffee shop in a
beautifully restored historic building. None of these businesses offers
anything that can't be bought at Walmart or online or by making
a short drive for flashier options in the city. But nevertheless, they
survive because local people continue to make the choice, daily, to
honor the implicit covenant of our residence and shop there. How

long can this covenant hold out against the cheap convenience of the Walmart? I honestly don't know, and there are some clear signs of decay in the proliferation of loan companies and weed shops. But I am going to stick with my end of the covenant and shop my main-street businesses for as long as the stores keep their end by keeping their doors open. This is about more than economics. It is about the common good.

Listening to The Cure in Chandler, OK

IT IS A LONG WAY from the sun-scorched Southern Plains of
Oklahoma to what I imagine as the dreary, rain-soaked landscape of
post-industrial England. Yet somehow, a decade before I ever crossed
the Atlantic, I managed to spend my teenage years in both. The world
around me was fence lines and haybales in all directions, but in my
headphones, and thus between my ears, reverb-soaked vocals over cold
synthesizers and chorus-laden guitar led me to the gray, industrial
city center of a nameless British city—maybe Manchester but maybe
totally imaginary. For me it was an escape. I didn't realize that the
post-industrial malaise in England was analogous to the culturally
deadening effects of the industrial agriculture that had been and was
continuing to replace our small family farms in Oklahoma. I didn't
notice that the poverty and desperation depicted in the music was
mirrored in the lives of the rednecks among whom I lived. The post-
punk English bands I loved were to me a thing sharply distinct from
the world I actually lived in. In my mind, the music was associated
with "getting out," with leaving my small hometown behind.

Sometime around my freshman year of high school, I stumbled
upon the Cure. The story is the same for many fans of the band:
I was an awkward kid with few friends, and the music resonated
with me in a way that mainstream music on the radio couldn't. I'd
read somewhere—most likely in a copy of *Spin* purchased at the

local grocery store—that the Cure is depressing, and depressing was what I wanted. A friend had gotten me into the Police, but I wanted something darker, something less prog and more Romantic. I thought I'd found it when I stumbled across the Cure's cassette single for the "Close to Me" remix in the electronics section of the Chandler, Oklahoma, Walmart, where I could only assume it had been shipped by accident. What I heard on that cassette once I was stretched out on the floor behind my closed bedroom door was far more infectiously giddy than I had anticipated. But I was instantly hooked on the weirdness and on the Romanticism of both the lyrics and the tendency toward lush and layered arrangements. It wasn't long before I fell headfirst into the *Disintegration* album: the emotion, the melodrama, the layers and layers of guitar and synth. I don't know if I knew the word *alienation* at the time, but I knew what it felt like. And now, thanks to the Cure, I knew what it sounded like.

About a year later I discovered Joy Division, a band perhaps even more depressing than the Cure. The first time I heard Joy Division, I was stretched out in the back of my parents' Ford Aerostar minivan. It was the summer after my sophomore year of high school, and we were on our way to New York City, a cross-country trek my family made several times. My sister, having just finished her freshman year of college in Arkansas, recommended we stop at a little record store near her campus. The store was called Electric Moo, and it was in Russellville, Arkansas. As I recall, it was a record store/headshop, and I believe it is now, sadly, purely a place to get vapes and pipes. It was the kind of funky place that inexplicably popped up like magic mushrooms in the nineties. Really it was the kind of place that popped up *with* magic mushrooms in the nineties. Something, maybe the simple gray cover, drew me to Joy Division's *Substance* album, a compilation of their best songs. I wasn't aware yet of all the lore surrounding lead singer Ian Curtis's suicide, but I had another vague impression of somberness and angst. That night, as my father drove us across Arkansas toward our first night's lodging in Memphis, I stretched out across a back seat of the van and stared upside down out a side window at the undiluted night sky with the *Substance* album in my Walkman. Because the music was at once sparse and cold yet also passionate and wounded, I fell in love with it immediately. A big part of the appeal was, of course, its difference from the music all around me—the Garth Brooks and Metallica that dominated rural high school in the nineties. It sounded smarter. It sounded wiser. It sounded like someplace else.

Over the next year, I bought a lot of black clothing.

There were other bands of course, some English but also some American. I especially loved the bratty and raucous honky-tonk-punk of the Replacements, and along with everybody else, I adored R.E.M. I liked the geeky weirdness of They Might Be Giants and the uber-coolness of the Stone Roses. I didn't abandon the Police and followed Sting into his solo career, even though harboring such super stardom in my cassette collection was a little embarrassing. Most of all, the Pixies offered an American version of the weirdness and alienation I craved, along with vaguely literary sensibilities. Still, Joy Division and the Cure were for me the pinnacle of meaningful music. They represented the outside and the beyond, everything not my little piece of earth in Oklahoma.

Soon my friendships began to revolve around the music. I'm not sure music is the marker of identity for young people today the same way it was in my youth. We staked our sense of self on the music we loved, and we sorted, categorized, and reduced others based on the music they listened to. Nothing was more indicative of a person's whole being than a concert T-shirt. The jocks and the normal kids listened to the radio. The stoners listened to metal and classic rock. And the artists and teenage intellectuals, my people, listened to the

Cure. We discovered that, if we parked in the lot of the burned-down grocery store in the evening, we could just pick up the alternative station out of Dallas. We discovered new bands. Nirvana was blowing up at the time, but I wasn't a big fan. They sounded crude and dumb to me. What I wanted to hear was the Cure and Cure-adjacent bands like Siouxsie and the Banshees, Echo and the Bunnymen, Concrete Blonde, My Bloody Valentine, and the Jesus and Mary Chain. I liked the Smiths a little bit, but not much. I wanted my music lush and velvety black. And I liked the few other people in my school who also liked their music that way.

The Cure are a pop band, in a sense, and they write songs about love. But even when a Cure song is about love it is also about death, loneliness, a sense of estrangement from traditional sources of meaning. On albums like *Faith*, Robert Smith explores overwhelming doubt and a sense of existential meaninglessness and dread. *Disintegration* chronicles both personal and cultural disintegration, and while *Wish* may have famously upbeat moments like "Friday I'm in Love," on the whole it is an album about coming to the end of hope. I arrogantly and stupidly thought no one in my hometown was thinking about these themes or dealing with these feelings. I utterly missed that what was so great in the music was that it captured nearly universal human experience so well. Instead, I held on to my trite and shallow idea that I was different and that, if I could only escape from this village of meatheads and rednecks, I would discover a place where my sensitivity and thoughtfulness would be truly appreciated. In the meantime, I attached myself to a small group of people I thought were also clear-eyed and thus outward bound.

Soon, predictably, we formed a band. I had played around with guitar for a couple of years, without progressing much, and had even had something sort of like a band with a friend, except that there were only two of us. When my new, mostly older, friends suggested

I trade in my guitar and join them on bass instead, I was more than willing. Three of us went together to a local music store in a nearby town and came home with matching black instruments: a Fender Squier Stratocaster for the lead guitarist, a Squier Telecaster for the rhythm-guitarist/vocalist, and a Squier Precision Bass for me. These were starter guitars, but I had never seen anything so utterly cool: all three matching and jet black with white pickguards.

These guys were, undoubtedly, the coolest people I had ever known. The lead guitarist was a musical genius and a pure Romantic poet at heart. He drove an old Mustang, and we spent hours in it. Some days we would drive around all afternoon looking for bandmates so we could organize a rehearsal, which is what one did in small towns before cell phones. Often, we would just drive around central Oklahoma intensely discussing music, poetry, and art, to the best of our under-developed abilities. He was a musically learned, skillful, and flamboyant guitarist who idolized Prince and later played in a couple of pretty well-known local bands. His tendency to quote *The Tempest*—"We are such stuff as dreams are made on"—gave me the distinct impression that our band was headed for legendary status, even though I knew that, in context, Shakespeare's words were really a gesture toward the vanity of life. The phrase "vain ambition" is not in a teenager's vocabulary, and perhaps it shouldn't be. If we overly check the absurd ambitions of the young, we risk steering civilization into a slough of stagnation and mediocrity. Midlife will provide ample opportunity to reflect on the emptiness of our grand ambitions. I am grateful to have spent my youth with other teenage Romantics.

Our drummer was a metalhead. Most drummers I have played with have been metalheads. The connection between love of heavy metal and the desire to rhythmically hit things is probably more a case of correlation than causation. He was, anyway, willing to play along, as long as we did something fast and loud occasionally. His grandmother owned the local music store, and she let us practice in the studio in the back. Coming from a musical family, he could play a number of instruments, and he went on to become a professional bassist who could play me under the table easily. We mocked his musical taste, but he knew what he was doing behind a set of drums.

Our keyboardist was the sort of kid who had taken piano lessons since the womb. He was also our high school's epitome of cool. His Stone-Roses-styled mop of hair was legendary, and he frequently attracted a small crowd of girls who wanted to touch it, much to my envy. His clothes were always years ahead. He was, in fact, so cool that he could have easily been mistaken for the biggest nerd in town, in his button-up rayon paisley shirts. His swirling, dark synth lines were exactly what we needed to get that post-punk sound.

The vocalist/rhythm guitarist, Eli, is the guy who is the biggest through line in my music "career" and in my life. He was later the best man in my wedding. He was a star in the high school choir, but he was also the quarterback on the high school football team. He was a standout on the baseball team as well as on the academic team. He could build anything, from homemade amplifiers to furniture, and he's now an ornithologist at a major research university. He's probably the best example of how this first band of mine was really a society of small-town geniuses. Well, of geniuses and me. I just tried to stay roughly in tune.

That summer, our heads full of big dreams, we drove four hours to Dallas to see the Cure on their *Wish* tour. It was everything I hoped it would be. For hours, including three encores, they played the music that mattered most to me. Robert Smith, with his wild hair and smudged makeup, seemed larger than life even from our fairly distant seats. He was the avatar of difference, of oddness, of everything I felt myself to be. I felt the music wash over me like a crashing wave on a moonless night, or that's how I thought of it at the time, anyway. The band ended the evening with "A Forest," a song that encapsulated the mix of alienation and Romanticism that made them the ultimate band for me. Drawing on myths and archetypes, Smith sings of running through a dark forest in search of an elusive lover whom he knows only as a voice or a vision. That sense of something beautiful and good that is always just out of reach and perhaps just an illusion, leaving me lost in the dark, pervaded my teenage years. We left Dallas more committed than ever to music and to weirdness. I left knowing that my return home was only temporary.

At the time, I thought our band might be my way out of my hometown. I was worried that I wouldn't be able to get the kind of scholarship I would need to afford college. In my addled teenage brain, a career in alternative rock seemed like a reasonable plan if the more conventional path out through education turned out to be closed to me. We played at the local pool hall, at parties, at a few all-ages venues, and once at a real club in Stillwater. I was sure these little gigs were just the prologue to our big "discovery." We hung around the Oklahoma music scene, sometimes even close enough to the Chainsaw Kittens, the Nixons, or the Flaming Lips to get a contact high. We made a demo, packaged it ourselves, and sold the cassettes on consignment at the record store in the mall in Shawnee.

But the big break didn't come. Soon, the keyboardist quit, and we had to get another drummer. We even played with a drum machine for a little while. We changed our name and spent a summer as a sort of "house band" at an all-ages club in downtown Shawnee, where we occasionally got into fights with local skinheads. Then the guitarist quit to pursue more likely avenues to musical success. Friends started going to college. After a while, it was just Eli and me left, so we convinced his cousin Aaron, another genius, to learn to play drums. When Eli came home from college the next summer, we carried on as a power trio and called ourselves "Flying Armadillo." We added a little acoustic guitar and harmonica to our songs about vampires. We started to sound a little like we belonged in Oklahoma.

But then I did go to college. Despite my shakiness in the STEM subjects, I was able to procure a full-tuition scholarship to a little liberal arts college in Arkansas. I no longer felt that my path out of Chandler was on a band tour bus. Flying Armadillo stopped playing together when Eli stopped coming home for the summer. I played in a couple of other bands in college, and even made a little beer money from it. Gradually, however, vain literary ambitions overtook vain musical ambitions. My goth-rock days seemed to be over. I even bought a few shirts in plaids and stripes.

But I was still listening to the Cure and Joy Division, though not exclusively of course. There was, in the mid-to-late nineties, an embarrassing jam band phase. Less embarrassingly, my studies helped me develop a taste for classical music and especially for jazz. I started to once again appreciate the music of my rural background, not the country music on the radio but the real thing: Hank Williams, Willie Nelson, and especially Johnny Cash. This was just in time for Cash's late-nineties final act, and "The Man in Black" provided me with a closer-to-home version of artistically expressed alienation. But always there was the post-punk; always there was the Cure. Sure, by my late twenties, I started to feel a little embarrassed about the juvenile Romanticism, all that angst and dark clothing and makeup. The music, however, always pulled me in. Strangely, in those years I was away pursuing my education, the music that had represented "getting out" and leaving home behind started to sound like home to me. I couldn't listen to *Disintegration* or *Substance* or any of the other albums without thinking of Chandler, Oklahoma, of the places I had first heard the music and of the people I had been with.

Maybe part of this association was simple nostalgia, but it was more than just that. All those days and nights of driving around listening to Robert Smith or Ian Curtis vocalize their aches and alienation had caused the music to soak into the landscape, to infuse my hometown with this melancholy music, at least in my mind. When I thought of the main street, lined with closed and empty shops at three in the morning, I thought of "Pictures of You" or "A Letter to Elise." When I thought about the patchwork of cow pastures and housing divisions rolling out in each direction from the city limits, I thought of "Atmosphere" and "Ceremony." The music had settled into the cracks. I was surprised to find out that this is what home sounds like.

And then I came home. Despite my overwhelming desire to shake the dust off my feet, I had married my high school girlfriend after college. She is the best thing to ever happen to me in my hometown and, no doubt, has a lot to do with redeeming the place in my estimation. When our first child was born, something clicked inside, and I knew it was time to go home. My resistance was simply gone. I wanted to belong to a place. I could finally clearly see the just claim that my hometown had on me. Within two years of finishing graduate school, I was back in Chandler jogging through the early-morning streets of my old neighborhood with "A Forest" in my earphones.

It took a while, but eventually we got the band back together, in its Flying Armadillo incarnation. With Aaron working as a lawyer for a local phone and communications company and Eli living in Norman and on the faculty at OU, making music together again seemed like the obvious thing to do. So we reconvened as a "dad band." Only now, we mixed banjo, mandolin, and sometimes even dobro into our sound. We leaned even further into the acoustic guitars, and once we started recording and gigging, we found ourselves generally classified as "alt-country." The label seems right: a mixture of "alternative" and down-home. In need of a project to occupy us during the depths of the COVID isolation, when we couldn't gig, we released a number of countrified covers of post-punk classics on Spotify, including a banjo-laden version of "A Forest." For me, creating this countrified version of a post-punk classic was a way of making peace between the version of me who yearned for something beyond small-town Oklahoma and the version of me who knows I belong here where my roots are. Sometimes a cover song can be the truest form of self-expression.

In "From the Edge of the Deep Green Sea," from the *Wish* album, Robert Smith sings about staying in a place forever. The lyrics implore us to raise our hands into the sky, and then rhyme that plea with a "goodbye" that will never be said.

I don't know if I will be here forever, but I have surrendered to being here for the rest of my life. I never thought that would be the case, in those days when I first heard the song. I assumed the place I would be spending the rest of my life was still to be discovered, that it was some better place, perhaps somewhere out there on the edge of the deep green sea. Instead, here I am surrounded by a sea of grass. When I put my hands in the sky, it will be the broad and infinite sky of the southern plains.

Ambiguity and Belonging under Friday Night Lights

I WAS A LITTLE bit relieved when the doctor told us the baby we were expecting, our first, is a girl. I didn't have anything against male babies. Certainly, it wasn't that I didn't want a son to continue the Myers family name. It wasn't even so much that I was intimidated by the average male infant's spraying capabilities during diaper changes. All things being even, I would have been indifferent to the sex of the baby and perfectly happy to embrace the clichéd "as long as it is healthy" line. All things, however, were not even. We live in the rural South, and with that comes, for every young man, expectations of athletic accomplishment. I knew that any son we had was likely to be judged by his ability on the wrestling mat, the basketball court, or—above all—the football field. I considered what I had to offer a son in genetic advantages and practical coaching, and I knew that his life would likely be hard.

I'm well aware of the challenges a woman can face in rural America. I know there is plenty of sexism and more than a little violence against women. But on the whole, I felt like I knew how to protect and correct for those problems. I'd seen my wife and sisters overcome those obstacles and thrive. I had no idea how to protect a son against the overwhelming expectation of athletic glory and the accompanying sense of utter irrelevance and insignificance if one turns out to be ungifted at and uncommitted to sports. When the entire culture around him seems to say that athletic achievement is what matters most, how could I protect a young man's delicate sense of self if he happened not to be physically competitive on the field? Could any amount of counter-programming at home cancel out the overwhelming volume from media, the culture, his teachers, and his peers, all constantly insisting in a myriad of subtle and not-so-subtle ways that glory in athletics is what gives a man dignity, status, and value? Or would the only thing to do be to take our newborn son and flee to some urban and northern environment where we would be strangers and sojourners, culturally at odds with those around us in so many ways, but free from the totalizing demands of the sports gods?

My fears were based in personal experience. Things didn't start out so badly for me; I grew faster than most of the boys in my class and was a standout at basketball, for a while. Back then, we didn't have elaborate travel leagues in every sport for children of all ages. We had city intramural sports in the summer and school sports during the academic year. My basketball career took off in middle school with several summers as low post for the "Celtics," as we called the intramural team assigned the green shirts. This was the age of Larry Bird, and—like his Celtics—we were rarely rivaled. I stood close to the basket and dropped in shot after shot over the heads of my smaller peers. I was fierce on rebounds as well. My parents sent me to basketball camps at nearby colleges, where I was drilled on the fundamentals of the game. By the time school sports started in junior high, I was ready to lock in a starting position. I held on to that position all the way up into my freshman year and the JV team. Then everybody else hit their growth spurts too. My stats fell, and I began to wonder if the temporary advantage in height was all I had going for me on the court.

Just as my basketball career was winding down, football was starting up. I took a try as both a tight end and a defensive end, since my small school didn't have enough players to dedicate each solely to offense or defense. I wasn't bad at defensive end, since I was fairly aggressive and reasonably quick. I wasn't bad, but I wasn't great either. My attempts on offense were worse. In short, I couldn't have caught the ball if it were the flu. It bounced off my hands, off my helmet, off my gut, and I was always left standing somewhere near the end zone staring at the ball on the ground. Our much more talented quarterback wisely stopped throwing to me.

I remember the game that finally drove home to me that I had reached the end of my athletic career. It was an away game with our biggest rival. I had missed the few passes thrown to me and had maintained my season-long habit of scoring no points at all. After the game, I changed quickly and was the first to sit down on the bus. Sitting there alone, I had what, looking back, could be called an epiphany: I am not an athlete. Through the bus windows, I could still see the stadium lights, but I felt a thousand miles away from the little cosmos they encircled. I've often cried at the loss of loved ones, and I cry easily when moved by poems, stories, and music. I can remember, however, crying only twice out of pure self-pity, both at reaching the ends of my own ability. The second time was at the realization that I would never be a professional musician; the first time was on that bus after the football game. Luckily, I had a very understanding and tender-hearted coach. Finding me on the bus, he offered me a cookie and a few words of encouragement, but he knew already what I had just discovered: that I was in the wrong place. I was held back by a general lack of talent and the right kind of physical development, sure, but I was also limited by a lack of motivation. I just couldn't find it in myself to care enough to put in extra practice and extra time in the gym. I half-heartedly finished

out the season, and when football season came the following year, I
signed up for an independent study on poetry in the school library.

As high school went on, I found myself increasingly indifferent to
sports, and thus I was greatly at odds with the little world of Chandler
High School. I'm sure my perception was exaggerated by my own
insecurities, but it seemed like practically everything around me cen-
tered on sports, and above all on football. Few of my peers or teachers
would have wanted me to feel small or unimportant, but the message
I was getting daily was that the only way to matter was to excel at
sports. In his Cultural Liturgies trilogy, contemporary philosopher
James K.A. Smith uses an Augustinian framework to understand how
our environments shape what we love. Smith refers to the practices
and discourses within our environments that mold our impressions
of what truly matters as "cultural liturgies." The liturgies of my high
school seemed to be primarily athletic. Each week was focused on
Friday's game, with decorated lockers by Wednesday, a pep rally by
late in the week, and a near suspension of all other school activity
on Friday. One could not imagine everyone's entire school week
focused on a choir concert or an academic team meet. Few people
at the school would have ever said that sports was more important
than anything else, even education, but they wouldn't have to put
it into words anyway. It was written into the school rituals. Did we
have rallies for the honor roll? Did we have parades for the choir?
The band supported the football team, but did the football team go
to band contests to cheer on their peers? There was a liturgy going
on all around us, and the hymns, the prayers, and the praises were
all to athletic prowess. I began to feel totally invisible.

I grew steadily more disaffected. I think I knew I was getting re-
sentful, but it felt so good to scoff and to snark about a culture that
loved "dumb jocks" more than anything else in the world. As I fell
more in love with great books and works of art, the sports-obsessed

world around me seemed more and more superficial and limited.
I still had a few friends that were athletes, but I didn't go to their
games. I dismissed the whole thing as trivial and as the world's
greatest example of messed-up priorities. While they rallied and
cheered, I sat in the library and read poetry.

It was a great relief to escape these sports-centered liturgies. I
spent a couple of summers at the Oklahoma Arts Institute, studying
creative writing in an environment in which I seemed to be admired
as much for my facility with iambic pentameter as our quarterback
back home was for his perfect spiral. Discovering a campus full of
writers, musicians, and actors who were not overshadowed by a larger
group of athletes but were, rather, performing their own art-focused
liturgies made me feel less like the invisible man. After graduation,
I chose to attend a very small liberal arts college. There were a few
sports teams there, but no one paid them much attention. I easily
spent four years without attending a single athletic contest and
without so much as ever hearing a report on wins and losses.

Yet I like sports. I certainly like a challenge, and I enjoy staying in
shape myself. I work out and run. I don't do these things competitively,
beyond the occasional 5K, but these are sports-adjacent hobbies that
have occupied a fairly central place in my life since college. Although
I spent many years hiding the fact from myself, I even like watching
sports. I had been enthralled with basketball in the age of giants:
Larry Bird, Magic Johnson, Michael Jordan. Later, when I was in
graduate school in St. Louis, an even earlier love of baseball returned
to me, as I got caught up in the excitement around Mark McGwire's
various runs at a home-run record. I became a Cardinals fan, along
with the rest of St. Louis.

I think that first summer and fall in St. Louis in the late nineties
was the first time I realized the role of sports in binding a community together. Sports has always been to me the thing that separates

me from most of the people around me, but now I could see it as something that could connect me to people with whom I might otherwise have little in common. If I happened to be stuck in traffic at the victorious conclusion of a game, I'd honk and shout along with everybody else and know that we had all been tuned in to the same broadcast. In between discussions of deconstruction and Russian formalism, I'd talk with fellow graduate students about last night's game. I'd chat about the postseason chances with the cashier when I stopped for milk on the way home. In the collegiate gothic halls of the university and in the big-box walls of the supermarket, I was part of one unified St. Louis. For the first time in my life, I had a subject for small talk. By the time our first child was born, in the midst of a good run at the World Series in 2004, I only half-jokingly suggested to my wife that we should name the kid "Albert Pujols Myers," regardless of the baby's sex.

By the time she was born, however, we had left St. Louis, and were already preparing to head home to rural Oklahoma. It was a relief to be returning home with a child who would have the option of participating in sports if she wanted but who wouldn't be consigned to invisibility if she didn't. She would be able to follow her own interests, without the heavy expectations of athletic glory. Within a few years, we had another daughter, and again there was the relief. It wouldn't matter if they were good at sports or not.

Those daughters both grew into first-rate band kids, and that is how I ended up attending high school football games for the first time since my freshman year so long ago. At first, of course, I went just to hear my girls play. It is hard, however, to completely ignore an entire football game happening directly in front of you. It is hard not just because the field is large and the game exciting but also because everyone around you is completely and simultaneously immersed in the game. Pretty soon, I was pulled in. I stood with the crowd and sang the fight song with the crowd. I leaned in at tense moments and jumped up at exciting ones. I was part of the liturgy. I came to appreciate the effort to play the game well, and I came to care when we won and when we lost. I noticed elements of the liturgy that weren't just about the athletes. There were, of course, the band and the rituals of fight song and, above all, of halftime. There were moments of conversation and connection with friends and neighbors during lulls in the game. There was one particular night when the game itself was overshadowed by a sudden flurry of thick and fluffy snowflakes such as are rarely seen in Oklahoma, and the entire stadium was swept up together into a moment of pure wonder. I am glad I was there.

What is the difference between invisibility and absorption into a whole? I'm not sure I know.

As real community is increasingly replaced by online abstractions or vague affinities of identity, I do know that our small towns can use just about anything that will hold them together with a sense of place and belonging. One would hope that there is more than sports to do that. A shared history and a shared sense of civic responsibility should hold us together. We should be bound by more rituals than those of the playing field, bonds forged in the local church and in the common interchange of life in commerce and in civil society. Yet sport, too, can do a lot to keep our sense of belonging intact. Loyalty to your local sports team is something visceral and instinctive, beyond the barriers of thought and culture that can interfere with other, though ultimately more important, communal bonds, such as faith. Sports cannot and should not be the beginning and end of our communal liturgies. Sports are not an ultimate or permanent end in themselves, and they cannot provide the basis for a meaningful life. A good game, however, can bring us all a little more together on a Friday night.

Still, I worry about the dominance of the sports liturgy in my little town. I drive down the street, and I see that the streetlights are decorated with flags in celebration of the football team. Local businesses show their community spirit by displaying posters of local athletes in storefront windows. Our dwindling county paper maintains a sports section; needless to say, there has never been an arts section. Most people my age spend their weekends driving their children to matches and tournaments around the state and into Kansas, Texas, and Arkansas. My fellow parents seem to have oriented their entire lives around the athletic careers of their twelve-year-olds, a liturgy that surely must communicate something to the child about what *really* matters in life. To attend our local high school is to *be* a "lion," whether or not you have ever represented that mascot on the court or field.

And now we have a son. He was born six years after we came home to Oklahoma, and he is twelve years old now, tall and thin like his father. He didn't start a basketball career early, like I did, but he does run cross-country. I don't know what pressures he is facing. He is a talented musician and has stuck with his piano lessons while also playing saxophone in the junior high band. One of his older sisters has already graduated, and the other will graduate in a couple of years. He will be there to take up their place in the high school band, excelling in the concert hall and in competition but also in the stands and at halftime on Friday nights. That is, unless he takes the field in helmet and pads instead of in feathered hat and marching shoes. Sometimes he mentions it, dropping into dinner conversation that he is thinking about playing football next year. He is more seriously considering basketball. I hope that if he does either of these things that it is because he enjoys them and because he finds them challenging and fulfilling, not because he is afraid he will fade into insignificance if he doesn't put points on the board. I don't know how to protect him from the pervasive cultural liturgy that surrounds us. I don't even know how to talk about it without my own baggage getting in the way.

On a recent evening my son and I play basketball after dark in the thin circle of light cast from the porch over our driveway. I worry he will get discouraged with consistently losing to me, but I haven't let him win so far. He is getting closer on his own, sometimes genuinely surprising me with a three-pointer from past the steps over by the parked car. He is not-so-gradually catching up to me in height. As we play, I think about how glad I am to have this game to give us something to connect through, beyond our mutual love of *The Simpsons* and of the all-meat pizza. As porch lights blink on all over town, I am sure we are not the only ones locally engaged in this father-son liturgy at the end of the work day. My rebound and my jump shot may be weighed down with all kinds of personal baggage, but I try not to pass that off to him. I'd like for him to love the game if he wants to love the game, to love the way it feels to run and to jump and to watch the ball fall through the net. I loved to play that way once, before a lot of other things got in the way. When we are called in to dinner, while he is putting the ball away in the garage, I say a little prayer under my breath that he will be truly a part of this place that is his home and that he will also be fully himself and know that he is seen and loved.

Part II

Tradition and Convention

I<small>T HAS LONG</small> seemed to me that we are overdue for an updated edition of Flaubert's *Dictionary of Received Ideas*. Flaubert's dictionary, published after his death, catalogs with rapier satirical wit those dumb things everybody says and nobody thinks about. In Jacques Barzun's translation, the entry for *Aristocracy* reads "Despise and envy it." For *Italy* he has "Should be seen immediately after marriage. Is very disappointing—not nearly so beautiful as people say." His definition of *workman* is "Always honest—unless he is rioting." His definition of *star* pokes fun at a persistent romantic individualism: "Every one follows his own, like Napoleon." Alas, his entry for *poetry* is "Entirely useless; out of date." That is a received idea with much too much staying power.

Many of Flaubert's entries are still relevant today, but we nevertheless desperately need an updated edition, because many of the stupid things "everybody" thinks and nobody thinks about have changed since Flaubert's time. The definition of *pipe* as "Not proper except at the seaside," for instance, might require substantial updating in the age of anti-tobacco campaigns, vaping, and legalized marijuana. *Students*, we might still agree, "never study," but no one could say it is still universally believed that they all "wear red berets and tight trousers," though I do believe the beret is due for a comeback.

It is not surprising that many of these received ideas have mutated or disappeared to be replaced by new ones since Flaubert's time. In fact it is the very nature of these things that they should change. In his book *Out of the Ashes*, Anthony Esolen provides a very useful rule of thumb: "If people have always said it, it is probably true; it is the distilled wisdom of the ages. If people have not always said it, but everybody is saying it now, it is probably a lie; it is the concentrated madness of the moment." One might think of this principle as privileging Chesterton's "democracy of the dead" over the democracy of the mere moment. Applying this rule to each opinion and position before adopting it is a good start on recovering one's sanity in an age of mass, conventional lunacy.

Flaubert's dictionary and Esolen's rule both prompt us to consider the very deep difference between tradition and mere convention. Much of what Flaubert catalogs is mere convention—widespread, sometimes persistent, but ultimately temporary rashes on the skin of human life. Tradition, contrastingly, is the skeletal structure that gives permanent and meaningful shape to life. To navigate life with sane prejudices—in the Burkean sense of *prejudice* as that judgment which we do not need to reinvent anew each time we utilize it—requires the ability to tell the difference between tradition and mere convention. A good education, one that includes the study both of great books and of logic, can go a long way toward developing this skill. A good education, wide reading, and sane conversation prepares one to hear the deep and abiding rhythm beneath the very catchy but ever-changing melody.

A sure sign of tradition, as opposed to mere convention, is the former's way of revealing a world not created or structured by our own preferences. Tradition tells us that we have responsibilities and obligations beyond those of our own choosing. We are not Goethe's Prometheus, nor are we the authors of ourselves, as Milton's Satan would claim. In a world not of our own making, responsibility, and obligation come to us unbidden and without our choosing. Tradition tells us that we are born into the rich web of an ordered creation, that we live not only as ourselves but as a son or daughter, a brother or sister, a father or mother, a parishioner, a citizen, a creature, a person living on a particular piece of earth. Through tradition, we discover who we are in relation to those who are around us, those who have gone before us, and those who will come after us. Tradition, though varied in its details and expression from place to place and time to time, thus connects the specificity of our time, place, and circumstance to a deeper current of permanence in all times and places. The idea of a permanent tradition, which we might associate with natural law and that is relevant to all times and places, in no way diminishes the beauty of the varied expressions of tradition in very particular times and places. The deep tradition is the trunk; the local tradition is the branch.

In Wendell Berry's short story "Fidelity," a dying man, Burley Coulter, is "kidnapped" by his own family and removed from the sterile and inhuman hospital so that he can die in contact with the particular piece of earth he loved. The authorities take exception to this removal and send Detective Kyle Bode to investigate. When Bode insists that the family had no right to simply remove Burley from the hospital, the family lawyer—a cousin and friend—responds, "Some of us think people belong to each other and to God." This is a succinct statement of what it means to live by tradition. The detective, by contrast, is a man who seems to belong only to himself—miserably so. Left empty after a failed marriage, Bode knows his life has gone wrong somehow, but he fails to see the answer in the deep belonging of the people he is investigating:

> He knew that she had not left him because she was dissatisfied
> with him but because she was not able to be satisfied for very

long with anything. He disliked and feared this in her at the
same time that he recognized it in himself. . . . And so perhaps
it was out of mutual dissatisfaction that their divorce had come,
and now they were free. Perhaps even their little daughter was
free, who was tied down no more than her parents were, for they
sent her flying back and forth between them like a shuttlecock,
and spoiled her in vying for her allegiance, and gave her more
freedom of choice than she could have used well at twice her
age. They were all free, he supposed. But finally he had had to
ask if they were, any of them, better off than they had been
and if they could hope to be better off than they were. For
they were not satisfied. And by now he had to suppose, and to
fear, that they were not going to be satisfied. He had become
almost resigned to revolving for the rest of his life, somewhere
beyond gravity, in the modern vortex of infatuation and divorce.

Without the gravity of traditional community with all its unchosen
obligation and responsibilities, Kyle Bode is left drifting alone. He
is Bowie's Major Tom.

Our current conventions in the modern Western world assure us
that our first responsibility is obviously to our own happiness and
that we can never be bound by that which we do not freely choose
from among numerous options, the way we choose our shampoo and
breakfast cereal. Thus the child who stays on the family farm or the
person who sticks out a difficult marriage—though only doing what
human beings have done for time out of mind—makes a choice that
is nearly incomprehensible to many people today. Why not just do
whatever makes you happy or appears to be in your own best interest? We've all become a version of Henry David Thoreau, who in
his famous essay "Resistance to Civil Government" brags of having
declared, "Know all men by these presents, that I, Henry Thoreau,

do not wish to be regarded as a member of any incorporated society which I have not joined." Thoreau's seemingly rugged individualism has become, by our time, thoroughly conventional.

In the modern world, utterly conventional people rarely recognize themselves as such. Most, in fact, would no doubt describe themselves as "free thinkers" and modern-day Thoreaus. It is conventional at this point in modernity to take dissent from long-established patterns of human life as a sure sign of intelligence and independent thought. Yet the point at which such free thought typically lands is the same well-worn ground as everyone else at the moment, or at least everyone they consider to be smart or well educated for the time being. In their "free thinking," the modern "rebel" tends to travel along certain predetermined channels of thought. Thus, questioning the conventions of the moment will quickly earn one a label of lunatic, idiot, or bigot. *Don't you know that there are more than two genders? Don't you know that the free market will solve all our problems? Aren't you aware that abortion is health care? Can't you see that America is God's chosen nation? Everybody knows this. Educate yourself. Free your mind, think for yourself, and load your Twitter profile with the same slogans and memes as everyone else.* It is hard not to think of Madeleine L'Engle's dark planet Camazotz, where all the children play in sync. It is convention, rather than tradition, that speaks in unison.

How much richer, wider, and indeed stranger is tradition. Tradition is almost never what any one of us would invent if left to ourselves. Tradition preserves the great mysteries on which human life is founded, and it invites us into those mysteries by calling us to live in deep relationship to realities not of our own choosing. When our lives are lived within a tradition, we cannot simply take the conventional idea of self-fulfillment or personal happiness as our guide. We must discern the good within a complex—one might say "ornate"—system of responsibilities and opportunities. This way of discerning the good is naturally deeper and more satisfying than conventional ideas of happiness. It is also more difficult, but the tradition itself provides the resources for this discernment, in the voice of the ancestors and in the preservation of "the best which has been thought and said," to borrow Matthew Arnold's famous phrase. While convention asks us to settle into a shallow rut, tradition calls us up, to shape our life in accordance with something bigger than ourselves and truer than our own preferences and guesses.

Tradition is not just ossified convention; rather it is the outworking in human cultures of an unchanging core at the heart of things. To honor tradition is not to live without change in a frozen state of suspension. It is to embrace a form of change that stays in orbit around an eternal fixed point, that providence of God which Boethius described as the fixed point of the turning circle. To put that another way, tradition is the unique working out in time and place of the eternal natural law. It is an incarnation of the unchanging. Thus tradition can thrive in a thousand varied expressions in a thousand times and places that all resound in rich harmony with the core music of truth, goodness, and beauty. Next to real tradition, convention is always monotone and boring.

Take for instance our current convention about the brevity of life as compared with the traditional treatment of the same subject. The slogan may have run its course of popular usage, but the convention of our times is still YOLO: "You only live once." And what does that mean? It means, apparently, do whatever you want to do whenever you want to do it. Max out the credit card and spend the week at Disney World. Have fun. Don't worry about obligations to the past or to the future. An age of consumerism and materialism tells you exactly what you would expect it to tell you about human life.

I do not mean, of course, that most people actually live in such a way. Some of us do "live in the moment" and reap the consequences, but most of us carry on with our daily responsibilities. Still, there is the lingering and nagging sense that we *should* be seizing the day. Current convention tells us that, were we living right, we would be living it up. We envy those without responsibility and without limits, and we fantasize about an untethered life. These fantasies occasionally lead one of us to throw off constraint, with predictably disastrous results for all involved. More often, however, we carry on in our limited life with the vague sense that we are doing it wrong. Convention tells us that we live only once and that we are messing up our one life by acting responsibly.

Much richer, deeper, and truer is the tradition's call to *memento mori*, remember your death. If YOLO is one shrill tone, *memento mori* is a complex chord on a pipe organ, with overtones, undertones, and harmonies. Sometimes these harmonies are reached only by the slow dissolving of apparent dissonances. The *memento mori* tradition contains the medieval monk's hopeful lifting of his eyes toward heaven, and it contains Hamlet's melancholic sense of despair. It subdues the classical pagan's *carpe diem* by means of the biblical injunctions to "redeem the time" and to "store up treasures in Heaven." YOLO takes all of three seconds to wrap one's head around, but to remember your death is a project of a lifetime, a project that requires both reading and stillness. To live within tradition is to spend years laboring to reconcile tensions and balance competing claims.

We can see the same contrast between conventional and traditional concepts of marriage. The conventional view of marriage in our time is that it exists primarily for the happiness and fulfillment of the included parties. This conventional view is enshrined in our movies, television shows, laws, and therapeutic practices. Its acceptance has, predictably, led to high rates of divorce. Indeed, the then-new belief that marriage is primarily about companionship was one reason the great English poet John Milton, perhaps among the first thoroughly

modern thinkers, argued for the legalization of divorce despite the
compelling, deeply moving, and traditional view of marriage he offers in *Paradise Lost*. Marriage as vehicle for personal happiness and
satisfaction is a long-standing convention in the modern world, and
that this convention was already being established in Milton's time
and was firmly in place by the nineteenth century explains the recent
rapid shift in the understanding of marriage among our politicians
and wider culture. We have collectively determined that marriage is
most obviously exclusively about the emotional and sexual satisfaction
of the involved parties. As much as progressives and conservatives
argue about the legalities of marriage, they don't seem to disagree at
all about its fundamental nature and purpose. Even many evangelical
Christians now think of marriage as primarily a way of ensuring
that one's own needs are met rather than as a way of stepping into a
timeless role that carries certain obligations and duties.

The traditional view, however, is again more complex, rich, and
beautiful. Traditional marriage includes the happiness of the bride and
groom, of course, but also much more. It often includes procreation,
naturally. As much as conventional thinking about marriage would
like to deny that fact, a survey of marriage outside of the modern
West will quickly reveal that the getting and raising of children has
universally been understood to be at the heart of matrimony, even
if not every good marriage is blessed with children. For we must
avoid the logical fallacy of assuming that any and all exceptions must
negate a rule. Traditionally, marriage includes also the bonding of
previously distinct families, "in-laws," into a web of social support.
This bonding of separate family bodies is another way marriage
forms the foundation of a stable society, as Cicero notes in his *De
officiis*. Moreover, marriage has been, and to some still is, a sacrament
of the church, and even when it is not seen in sacramental terms,
it is still seen as an event at the heart of the communal life of the

congregation. Throughout the New Testament and the Christian tradition, marriage is an image of Christ and his church. Marriage is famously the culmination of Shakespeare's comedies, and these great plays tend to end with marriage because it is the personal and local embodiment of the *concordia discors* that holds the world together, an affirmation that there is, indeed, a binary at work in the fabric of reality. Traditionally, marriage is a deep mystery at the heart of the mundane world.

My purpose here is not to defend, or even fully define, the traditional view of marriage. It is only to point out that the tradition is something that requires more thoughtful engagement than does current convention. The convention is always near at hand: in the pop culture we breathe in throughout our waking hours, in the slogans we mindlessly repeat as conversation, and in our dominant forms of education. This is, in fact, the biggest challenge faced by defenders of tradition: often the arguments against tradition come out of convention and are thus glib, superficial, and easy to both express and to grasp, while arguments for tradition take patience, reflection, and effort. It is easy to articulate why tearing down the cathedral to build a super highway will relieve traffic congestion and thus improve commerce, and convention tells us that the practical economic good must come before "merely aesthetic" considerations. Traffic statistics and studies of "economic impact" can be produced to tell us all what we already know: that the old must always give way to the new. Understanding why the cathedral should stand even if very few ever enter it for either worship or tourism asks a lot more of us, both in time and effort, as it asks us to think about the value of the past as well as the relationship between beauty and value. When arguments are to be made and understood, convention springs to service unbidden; tradition must be worked for.

A sense of tradition is built either through a long commitment to a place and a people or through a true liberal arts education. Ideally, it is built through both. Conventional thinking is a lot like a bean-bag chair: it is easy to get into, but getting out of it requires a helping hand. One of the primary purposes of education today must be that helping hand. A liberal arts education should equip students to discern tradition from mere convention. It can do this by immersing the students in the great books and in study of the human condition throughout time. In reading widely, the students will not encounter simple agreement on big questions. They will encounter much disagreement and diverse views of life. But in the midst of the great conversation, there emerges a broad consensus about the nature of human life as well as certain threads of truth to be traced through the writings of the past. Students can learn a lot about what sets mere convention apart from real tradition simply by learning what are the truly worthwhile questions to ask about human life. They can also benefit greatly simply from encountering with sympathy and open-mindedness wise voices from the past that contradict current convention. They at the very least can see across the centuries of the human record a clear picture of what to reasonably expect from human life, and this is often enough to clear away the smog of conventional thinking.

Convention is not limited, of course, to leftist or progressive ways of thinking. The temptation to default to the conventional is a fundamental aspect of our shared human frailty. There is much conventional thinking among the American right, often on economic issues, for instance. This has been especially true as American conservativism has become entangled with classical liberalism and its postmodern offspring, libertarianism. Yet I prefer to think of "conservativism" as a philosophy of life rather than as a political ideology, which is why I continue to call myself a conservative despite the damage done to the label by many of those who claim it. A true conservativism in the Burkean tradition is about peeling away convention to get to the solid rock of tradition. With all due respect to William F. Buckley Jr, the conservative must do more than stand athwart history yelling "stop." Freezing things at any particular point in time would only fossilize the conventions of the moment. We should aim to conserve what is deepest and true, not just what happens to have immediately preceded the present. It should be the conservative's task to reconnect the manner of our lives and the institutions of our civilization—schools, colleges, churches, governments—to the solid truths beneath the surface, peeling away the layers of mere convention to find the permanent things. It is our task to hear, and to point the ears of others toward, the deep and abiding rhythm beneath the constantly changing melody.

The Christian University: Steward of Western Civilization

FOR MANY AMERICANS, the onset of fall means pumpkin-spice lattes and cozy sweaters. For some it means football, and for others it means hayrides. For me, for my colleagues, and for five hundred or so sophomores at our university, it means Dante's *Divine Comedy*. In early October of each year, we make our pilgrimage with the great medieval poet through Hell, up Mt. Purgatory, and into the highest Heaven. Our annual reading of the *Divine Comedy* is a central part of the core curriculum at our Christian liberal arts university. This journey is nearly as arduous as the pilgrim Dante's guided tour of the afterlife. Why do it? With students increasingly majoring in preprofessional programs that demand ever more credit hours to satisfy accrediting agencies and professional bodies, how can we justify giving so much time to the study of the great books of the Western world, reading the works of Homer, Sophocles, Shakespeare, Milton and many more? Under pressure from a culture that demands college lead directly to financial stability, how can we justify a core curriculum so extravagantly "impractical" and backwards looking? In an age in which "diversity" has become the supreme value in higher education, how can we justify devoting so much time solely to the West and the "dead white men" that are supposedly at its center? Simple. A robust education in the cultural foundations and traditions of the Western world is the only way to rescue students from the chronological provincialism that so severely stunts contemporary hearts and minds, a goal that should be a first priority for a Christian institution of higher learning. We read old books in order to teach students *not* to "live in the moment" but rather to dwell in a rich garden.

Imagine a beautiful garden in the midst of a gray, industrial, bleak city. The city's architecture is functional only, given totally to the making of money or to the most ephemeral, when not downright base, forms of entertainment. This city is all big box store and mega-super-cinema-plex, concrete blocks, steel, glass, and garish neon lights arranged along endless strips of gray interstate. But the garden is lovely, lush, and inviting. It is full of beautiful growth and well-crafted stonework. It has broad lawns and quirky nooks. It provides both shade and light. It is a place for true recreation and joyful exercise. And it is ancient, passed down through generations of city-dwellers as a place of relief and regeneration. What would you think of the generation that let that garden die through neglect? What would you think of a people who intentionally destroy it?

The main reason Western civilization, with an emphasis on Great Books and the history of ideas, deserves a prominent—indeed, *the* prominent—place in the curriculum of the Christian university is stewardship. And we might call stewardship, in light of the cultural mandate received at our original creation in the garden, simply *cultivation*. In Western civilization, we have inherited a garden full of wisdom—and a few thorns—and it is incumbent upon us to maintain and cultivate it for the wisdom, even if we must warn visitors to be careful of the thorns. Following in the footsteps of the ancients, medieval Christian philosophers identified three "transcendentals" that point us toward God: the True, the Good, and the Beautiful.

We study the history and literature of Western civilization in order to see these transcendentals at play in our own cultural heritage; to appreciate the ways in which those who came before us have striven for the True, the Good, and the Beautiful; and to better understand how that quest for transcendence has been limited and impinged upon by sin and the reality of a fallen world. We study Western civilization because there is much in it that is edifying and because there is much in it that is tragic. This study is how we lay claim to our rightful inheritance of wisdom, nobility, and gracefulness. As Michael Oakeshott says, "Every human being is born an heir to an inheritance to which he can succeed only in a process of learning."[1] Through study, we become stewards and cultivators of our culture.

Of course, we want the garden to be there should anyone wish to recreate in it, but we also want it to be there because we know that keeping a garden in the midst of the city nudges the whole city, if only slightly, garden-ward. The very existence of a garden at the center of a city can subtly change the character of that city. The city that makes room for a garden in its center makes room for flower boxes in its windows and even trees along its streets. Perhaps it is impossible to provide a robust cultural education for all students at all institutions. That impossibility, however, should not cause us to demolish the whole garden. Its beauty, if left intact, will spread outward. The exercise some receive there will make them examples to others to pursue such exercise as is possible in their part of the city. Only a society of utter barbarians would destroy a beautiful garden simply because "not enough people" could avail themselves of it. Someone has to keep the garden, even when most people are unaware of or indifferent to its existence.

The value of the garden is most apparent in its perennials and in its old stonework. If we view Western history as a civilization's strug-

---

1. Michael Oakeshott, *The Voice of Liberal Learning* (Liberty Fund, 2001), 37.

gle—full of both triumph and failure—to attain to Truth, Goodness, and Beauty, then it is most valuable when study of it is both deep and long. Students need exposure to the long, if cracked then fairly unbroken, chain of thought, feeling, and experience we call "Western civilization." No other course of study so cures them of chronological provincialism, so saves them from being what Edmund Burke called "the flies of a summer." This ability to dwell in the fullness of time is surely part of what our Creator wants to encourage in us when, generations after the men He is referring to lived, He described Himself to Moses as "The God of Abraham, Isaac and Jacob" (Exodus 3:15). Recalling this phrase, which appears several times in the Old Testament, Jesus himself tells us "He is not the God of the dead but of the living" (Matthew 22:32). For those who take seriously the resurrection of the dead and the biblical view of time, the past is always present. Failing to see the present in terms of the past is failing to see at all.

Of course, this wider perspective enables the student to think about contemporary problems with a greater perspective, but perhaps more importantly, it also uncramps their souls. Knowledge of Western civilization—a true knowledge of its change and continuity over time—gives the student room to breathe intellectually, morally, spiritually, aesthetically, and emotionally. It frees the student from the tyranny of the moment, from merely fashionable, inevitably superficial ways of being in the world. Life in the fullness of time is a life more abundant than living in the prison of the moment.

A hodge-podge of "cultural credits" sprinkled as a concession throughout an otherwise utilitarian education will not accomplish this goal of transforming students into citizens of what G. K. Chesterton famously called "the democracy of the dead." This transformation from an inhabitant of the narrow moment to a dweller in the fullness of time takes an experience we might call "immersive." It takes semesters of study in a coherent and contiguous plan. The study of the West, when done chronologically through deep reading of great books, offers this.

Students, and everyone else, should, of course, learn about other cultures. Let them take classes on Buddhism in India, on Tang Dynasty Chinese poets, on the Mali Empire in Africa. There is much that is edifying, instructive, and fascinating in those subjects. But let these studies be in addition to, not at the expense of, the sustained, robust, multi-semester study of the West. A perhaps well-meaning curriculum committee will inevitably cheapen the noble goal of exploring world cultures by pretending that three hours in Polynesian folklore is as good as fifteen hours in Western Civilization, and many less well-meaning academic institutions really just want to open up twelve more hours for the study of management or sports nutrition and see "multiculturalism" as a convenient hammer with which to smash the rigorous core curriculum they think is standing in their way. If, however, we think about the subject for a moment, we will see that it is obviously not a question of "Western Civilization versus World Civilization." There is no "world civilization," and trying to offer it as an alternative to study of Western civilization just means cutting up the world's many fascinating and deep civilizations into a reductive smattering of offerings competing for the student's attention. Is it somehow better, in the name of equity, to do an injustice to five civilizations within our core curriculum rather than do a reasonable amount of justice to one? Only Kurt Vonnegut's Diana Moon Glampers, the handicapper general of his story "Harrison Bergeron," would think so.

Of course, one might then say why not develop a deep sense of time by offering a fifteen-hour core in say, Chinese civilization or Indian civilization or African civilization? In which case we instantly see the absurdity in asking all students, as opposed to only majors in comparative literature or anthropology, at an American university to devote such a huge amount of time to a civilization that does not constitute the immediate context of the educational institution in which they are studying. In other words, Western Civilization belongs in the core because this is the West. The Western tradition gave rise to the university as we know it. The Western tradition also gave rise to the political world as we know it. As Russell Kirk pointed out in his *Enemies of the Permanent Things*, one very good reason to study the Bible, Cicero, Virgil, Shakespeare, and others is that our founding fathers studied them and utilized what they learned there in framing the republic that is our political heritage. In the West, our political foundations, our artistic foundations, and our theological foundations are rooted in the great conversation we call the Western tradition. If we do not know this tradition, then we do not know ourselves and truly are "the flies of a summer." A Christian university ought to take as a primary goal the restoration of the resources of Christendom—intellectual, spiritual, and aesthetic—to a church too often imprisoned in the trends of the moment.

At a Christian university, we encourage students to live fully in time because the story of Western civilization is largely the story of the rise, triumph, and decline of a distinctly Christian culture. A good study of Western civilization begins with a thorough study of Greek and Roman antiquity, along with a thorough reading of and study of the Old Testament and its people. The student cannot understand the meaningful synthesis of the Christian and classical worlds unless he has a thorough understanding of antiquity on its own terms. Additionally, seeing the thoughts and questions of the church anticipated by Socrates and Sophocles, for instance, is a powerful lure out from the narrowness of the moment to gain a better perspective on the fullness, the awe-inspiring breadth of God's truth. Overall, we cannot understand the human condition into which Christ is incarnated if we do not look deeply into the Greek and Roman past.

Then the student is ready for the early church, the Middle Ages, the Renaissance, and Reformation. To study these things is for the Christian student to see what the church, what the coming of Christ, has wrought not just in the individual spirit but in the whole of a cultural unity we call "the West." From there, the student turns to the "Enlightenment," modernity, and postmodernity to form a solid understanding of Western culture as, in C. S. Lewis' phrase, "post-Christian." The only way to grasp and wrestle with the secularization of our culture is to study the developments in thought, art, and technology that encouraged the disenchantment of the modern world.

None of these important goals can be met if we treat the core curriculum as something to do with our "left-over" hours. If a Christian university cannot manage a robust core in the great tradition while it meets the demands of professional programs, then it is obligated to abandon those professional programs. I suspect, however, that even the smallest Christian school can manage to provide both a solid and rigorous core education and a good preparation for honest work in particular lines of vocation. It is a matter of not letting one aspect of the education, almost always the practical side, overwhelm the other, often done in the name of "compromise" until the core is whittled down to an anemic smattering of electives. The world, indeed, needs nurses, engineers, and lawyers; and it will, with or without the Christian university, have them. It also needs men and women of sensibility, people who dwell in the fullness of time, and these it is unlikely to have without institutions of higher learning firmly committed to the Christian intellectual tradition and to the serious stewardship of the cultural past and present. When the Christian university spends its time and resources scuttling after utilitarian, materialist educational trends, we trivialize our important role as stewards of the culture. We fail in our duty to care for "the permanent things." When we rise to meet that duty, however, we provide the world not only with teachers of Great Books but also with liberally educated nurses, lawyers, accountants, and engineers. We provide the world with thoughtful and rational people in any profession that is good for a lover of Christ to follow.

Our students come to us from all around the country and from across the world, from big cities and small towns. Almost all of them, however, are chronologically provincial. They are living in the moment merely because they have been given no greater dwelling to inhabit. If we are to do what we say we will—which is to educate them—then we must broaden their sense of time so that they may spread out in mind and spirit. We must make available for them the cultural and intellectual heritage valued by every learned person in the West up until the postmodern age.

In the *Divine Comedy*, Dante is not sent alone into the afterlife. He has Virgil, the great Roman poet, to guide him. Virgil comes to him in the dark woods in which Dante is lost. Let us pray that it won't be at such a lost and dangerous moment that the guidance of the past comes to us. Not all pilgrims who wander into the woods come out again. Let us offer our students a garden in which to meet Virgil. We owe them such instructive and enriching friendships with the dead.

How Liberal Arts Colleges Could Save Civilization

UNDER PRESSURE from campus progressives, Loyola University Maryland removed Flannery O'Connor's name from a residence hall. Another Jesuit school, Canisius College, has conceded to a more utilitarian form of erasure and eliminated its classics program while beginning steps to "streamline" its core curriculum. Small liberal arts colleges around the country are renaming buildings, removing statues, and "modernizing" curricula. These are not unrelated phenomena. Nor are these educational losses unrelated to the general destruction and desecration in several major American cities in recent history. We might call it all "the spirit of oblivion."

The same desire to "burn it all down" is increasingly applied to banks, books, and bourgeois norms throughout the West. Businesses are smashed, and curricula are slashed. All are instances of the zeitgeist's mad rush toward amnesia and oblivion. We seem to be living in a culture determined to reduce time down to the narrowest, most confined version of the mere moment. Many people seem to think the antiquity of any institution or structure is reason enough to torch it. Recently, I can peruse neither the pages of *The Chronicle of Higher Education* nor of any more general news periodicals without thinking of the closing words of Alexander Pope's *Dunciad*:

Lo! thy dread Empire, Chaos! is restored;
Light dies before thy uncreating word:
Thy hand, great Anarch! lets the curtain fall;
And Universal Darkness buries All.

The same love of darkness which will tear down statues, regardless
of who they depict, will sacrifice the liberal arts core of education in
the name of "relevance" and "best practices." The culture wars are not
really about right versus left; they are about memory versus oblivion.

Regardless of one's party affiliation, one is either with the forces
of memory or with the forces of forgetting. There is a battle in the
Western world over the continuation of Western civilization, a battle
between those who would *remember* because they understand that
memory sustains civilization and those who would forget for the very
same reason, those who hope that forgetting our past will usher in
a permanent utopia, a "no place" that is also a *utempia,* a "no time."
One side offers continuity based on a rich cultural inheritance. The
other side offers a capitulation into darkness and barbarism.

In a sense that actually has only very little to do with party affiliation, we might call these groups "conservatives" and "progressives,"
as long as it is understood that one frequently may meet with very
progressive-minded right-wingers driven by a thoroughly utilitarian
view of the world and the idolization of "progress." Such nominal conservatives are generally in favor of preserving "family values" though
unclear on why it is important to do so and incognizant of the cultural
conditions that make family possible. One even meets the occasional
leftist conservative, a generally amiable, and often academic, type
who is all for taxation, big government, and the sexual revolution, as
long as no one touches the Shakespeare requirement in the English
major. In fact, many people unknowingly straddle the line between

the party of remembering and that of oblivion. Yet in our cultural battles, those lines seem to be drawn ever more sharply as the forces of social media and tribal thought push us into extremes. We have come to a point at which our nation's liberal arts colleges, particularly our few remaining Christian liberal arts colleges, must consciously and explicitly choose between these two sides of the memory line.

If the liberal arts college doesn't do the work of remembering, then who will? We may continue to have a strong slate of research universities, public and private, dedicated to the generation of new knowledge, but who will preserve what has already been known for centuries and millennia? The unique role of the scholar is to remember. That is what distinguishes the scholar from the scientist, whose concern is primarily with the advancement of knowledge. Inasmuch as a scholar innovates, he does so in order to preserve, as the Renaissance humanists advanced our understanding of classical Latin and ancient texts in order to recover and preserve the past. The scholar is thus very distinct from the scientist. In modern education we have confused these two roles, and the result is the proliferation of bad "scientists" in the humanities, ever more desperately fumbling after some new take on their "fields." If you doubt this, spend an hour or two at any academic conference in the humanities. In pursuing the latest trends and developments—and the notoriety and grants that go with them—the liberal arts college finds itself at odds with its core identity, which is essentially conservative in the truest meaning of that word.

As Michael Oakeshott makes clear in *The Voice of Liberal Learning*, the essence of the liberal arts is not in being "well-rounded" by taking a smattering of unconnected and arbitrary classes, nor in merely fostering "critical thinking"—which often means simply learning to ape the opinions and beliefs of the professor—but rather in the reception of an inheritance. This inheritance enables us to be more than well-rounded; it prepares us to be more fully formed. It fosters something greater than critical thinking; it fosters the use of reason and the recourse to the resources of the great tradition. A good liberal arts education requires the kind of cultural memory preserved in a strong core curriculum. The inherently conservative goal of a liberal arts education is to form students into the kind of people who can think *for* themselves but who would never be so ignorant and shallow as to attempt thinking *by* themselves. The educated person thinks along with such minds as Plato, Augustine, and Locke, disagreeing and agreeing as reason and love of the good provokes. The educated person doesn't need to reinvent the world every five minutes but rather thinks alongside the great minds of the past.

Yet the progressive and instrumentalist ethos of the moment rejects out of hand the insights of the *mos maiorum*, the way of the fathers. An indifference from many on the right to the permanent things—which James Matthew Wilson in his *The Vision of the Soul* has traced to a strategic shift among conservatives toward an almost exclusive focus on economics during the Reagan years—has left culture in the hands of the left, who have not stewarded it well. The culture wars reveal that the right has for too long been indifferent to the inheritance of Western culture and the left has been forthrightly antagonistic to it. Meanwhile, a shrinking handful of liberal arts colleges have continued to pass on the inheritance of Western civilization through robust and coherent core curricula. Such colleges, however, are few in number, though they tend to thrive while their more utilitarian and trendy peers strain and fold.

Despite the growing prominence of classical education in the K–12 world and the clear success of many Great Books colleges, small liberal arts colleges now more than ever face a pressure toward cultural oblivion, a pressure to abandon their core principle of re-membering. My colleagues in the liberal arts sometimes speak loftily of remaining "above the culture wars," but they have failed to realize that the war has come to us. Appeasement is no longer feasible. If one teaches Old Testament or European history or Shakespeare, then one's classroom is the frontline. A growing number of progressives see the very act of teaching Homer or T.S. Eliot as inherently political, and unacceptably so. The chant of Jesse Jackson at Stanford back in the 1980s—"Hey hey, ho ho, Western Civ has got to go"—has only grown over the past thirty years from a commentary on curricula to what is nearly a statement of a negative metaphysics. It is a death wish for a civilization, and it is a widely shared sentiment. The forces of amnesia will not be satisfied until all traces of the past have been eliminated so that their utopia of the summer fly may be established. If a college is going to hold the line against oblivion, from now on it will require a great deal of courage and conviction. It will also require the generous support of those who oppose the amnesiac agenda.

Educating in the tradition of the Christian West has always been a matter of remembering, a vision articulated by Hugh of St. Victor, Cardinal John Henry Newman, Christopher Dawson, and many others. A commitment to memory in the face of oblivion entails a strong and sizable core curriculum rather than a smattering of unrelated "electives" or a small collection of "general ed" requirements that are there merely to be gotten out of the way. This is so because to assert that memory matters is to assert that the contents of memory, the things to be remembered, matter. Liberal arts education is about learning to think, but it is also about preserving the things worth thinking about.

A true liberal arts core curriculum preserves the ethos of the classical liberal arts not by preserving the medieval *trivium* and *quadrivium* in amber but rather by carrying on the essential mission of the seven liberal arts in the Western university: the transmission of a cultural heritage. In studying grammar, rhetoric, and logic, the original liberal arts students encountered the best minds of the past and kept them alive in their own minds. In studying arithmetic, geometry, astronomy, and music, they kept alive the great tradition of reason's place near the center of Western civilization and of the wondrous relationship between reason and beauty. Until very recently, education was conceived of throughout the Western world as an inheritance.

Such a mission does not dictate a seven-course core corresponding exactly to the seven liberal arts of tradition, but it does dictate that certain types of courses form part of the modern liberal arts core. Ideally, there will be ancient languages: Hebrew, Greek, and Latin. If these languages do not live in our Christian liberal arts colleges, they will be dead languages indeed. There should be courses covering the history and literature of the Western world from Ancient Greece through the twentieth century. Such courses will take several semesters to complete, but neglecting such study is to shirk our responsibility for keeping what has been passed down to us. There must, of course, be core courses in the Bible, so that the student comes to understand not only that great text itself but also the rich theological traditions that come out of it. Additionally, if our purpose is rooted in remembering, the Christian liberal arts college would be wise to add courses in historical theology and in the founding principles of the American republic. There must be courses in philosophy and logic to introduce students to the big questions that have driven human thought and to the tools used to address those questions. There also must be courses in mathematics and science, courses geared not primarily toward producing new professional mathematicians and scientists but rather toward initiating students into the understandings of abstract reason and of empirical investigation that have played a crucial role in Western epistemology. Such a curriculum is the spirit, if not the letter, of the *trivium* and the *quadrivium*, and the college that opposes oblivion makes such a core its top priority as well as the center of its identity.

Additionally, the church would do well to remember that supporting liberal arts colleges is the best chance at preserving a culture in which religious liberty is preserved. The integration of the Christian faith and the Western political tradition has resulted in the freedom of conscience that allows the church to continue to preach. Maintaining this political legacy of freedom requires a substantial population that understands the road that runs through Jerusalem, Athens, Rome, and London. It requires an understanding of Athenian Democracy, the Magna Carta, the Glorious Revolution, the Federalist Papers, and much more. If our citizens have no concept of where religious liberty comes from and of the intellectual conditions that lead to its establishment throughout the West, we have little hope of preserving that liberty for long. It—along with other important political, artistic, and cultural traditions—will fall into the darkness about which Alexander Pope warns us in his bleak prophecy.

Twenty-five years ago, Thomas Cahill surprisingly landed on the bestseller lists with his *How the Irish Saved Civilization*. He argued that the Irish monasteries preserved the cultural inheritance of the West during the barbaric darkness of the early Middle Ages. It was, to a great extent, the monks secluded in the monasteries of Europe who kept safe the cultural treasures of antiquity for later revival. If we are on the verge of a new kind of "dark age"—one that may be rich in technology and comfort and is yet still darkened in its understanding—then one must wonder who will save civilization this time. Who will keep the past secure, even if sequestered. It may just have to be our liberal arts colleges.

How the Small Liberal Arts College Can Thrive

MANY AMERICAN colleges are doomed to close in the near future. Even before the COVID-19 crisis, experts were predicting that a quarter, a third, or even half of small colleges in America could close due to demographic change and financial failure in the coming decade. The pandemic has certainly escalated that concern. Why would students continue to pay significant money for an education delivered online, especially when they can get a similar Zoom education much cheaper from nearby state universities? Even as most colleges return to something like normal operations, students are left with lingering doubts about the value of what some might call "the whole college experience."

Large state universities may limp by on taxpayer money; certainly, prestigious Ivies and research institutions will glide through on the strength of that prestige and their sizable endowments. Smaller private colleges, however, are often nearly entirely dependent on student tuition, and thus they live and die by enrollment numbers. Even before the pandemic, as many as six out of ten colleges missed their enrollment goals for 2020. Everybody knows that the little colleges that dot the nation are in trouble.

Except Christendom College reported record applications and

campus visits in 2020 despite the pandemic conditions that were drastically affecting enrollment elsewhere. Except Hillsdale College has continued to admit classes that break records both in size and in academic achievement. Except as decline was setting in elsewhere, the University of Dallas set an institutional record for enrollment in 2018 and has not declined significantly since then, despite the pandemic.

What do these small colleges have in common? They are all committed to teaching the Western tradition with depth and rigor. The honors program at Oklahoma Baptist University, a Great Books program which focuses on study for wisdom and virtue and which I direct, had its biggest enrollment ever in the fall of 2020 and continues to admit around fifty new students each fall. These are early signs of coming success for colleges that are willing to double down on their identity as liberal arts institutions unashamedly teaching the Western tradition. It may seem counterintuitive to some, but the path to stability and even growth for small colleges is the road less traveled of traditionalism.

By traditionalism, I mean a faithfulness to the liberal arts tradition, including a commitment to teaching the history, art, and thought of Western civilization. While many schools still claiming the liberal arts mantle are dropping programs in humanities and cutting their core curricula to appeal to a broader spectrum of students, there is little reason to suspect that the general population of students will be lining up to pay more for the same watered-down education they can get at state universities or online.

Gutting the liberal arts certainly has not saved struggling institutions from increasing financial woes, as we continue to hear news regularly of colleges forced to shut the doors for good. Many colleges seem to suspect that a real liberal arts education is too hard of a sell to the general public and hope to survive by replacing core curricula with cafeteria-style options that are either more "practical" or more political. Such compromising colleges are, of course, right that the vast majority of Americans are not interested in rigorous, deep education in the liberal arts tradition. But they are dead wrong in thinking that the key to survival is appealing to the majority of Americans. Small liberal arts colleges can thrive with a fraction of the market share. But ironically, many are missing out on the small percentage of students they need by attempting to cast a broad net to catch the general populace.

The major trend in America may be, as always, toward dumbing down and bland mass culture, but there is a strong minority trend emerging as a quest for meaning and depth. Some people are sick of being spoon-fed from an endless buffet of triviality and sordidness. Whether or not you find their arguments convincing, the popularity of neo-Stoic gurus like Jordan Peterson suggests a sizable number of Americans are looking about for some sense of purpose and meaning, grabbing on to anything that sounds at least more profound than the pop culture mainstream. Stoicism is trending. The sacralization of politics, so evident in our public life, might also be slight, sad evidence of this search for significance; those with no real eschaton will find something already immanent to take its place. A revolt against the age of superficiality is brewing, and while it may be small, it will not be insignificant.

The best indication of the spreading desire for a deeper vision is the rapid expansion of classical schools in K–12 education. "Classical education" is a growing movement in pre-college education in which educators, students, and parents reject the utilitarianism governing modern education and seek a return to traditional liberal arts principles. Often modeling their curricula on Dorothy Sayers' essay "The Lost Tools of Learning," classical schools focus on the *trivium* of the medieval university: grammar, logic, and rhetoric. While they do not neglect science, classical schools strongly emphasize the humanities, particularly classical languages, history, and literature. Classical schools generally share a commitment to human dignity, an insistence on the existence of objective truth, and a sense of stewardship for the Western tradition of thought and culture. They teach their students to read books and to love wisdom, making them perfect potential students for the handful of true liberal arts colleges left.

And there are a lot of classical schools. As far back as 2015, John J. Miller reported in *National Review* on "the resurgence of classical education." It is a story of rapid expansion, indicating a widespread desire among parents to give their children an education more meaningful than what most public schools can provide. According to the Gospel Coalition, between 200,000 and 300,000 American students from kindergarten through high school were receiving a classical Christian education by 2017. And the classical explosion is not only a Christian phenomenon. Bobby Goodrich is a national recruiter for Great Hearts Academies, a network of classical charter schools in Texas and Arizona. He says that Great Hearts has grown over the last fourteen years to twenty-nine schools with 17,500 students in Arizona and Texas; they have as many students on their waiting list as they have currently enrolled and expect continued high rates of growth. Thales Academy, a private and secular school with campuses in North Carolina, Tennessee, and Virginia, has over 3,600 students and continues to grow.

These numbers may be small compared to the number of students in regular public education around the country, but a liberal arts college with five hundred to five thousand students needs to capture only a small number of the young people graduating each year. A smart small college can capture all the tuition it needs by appealing to classical schooling families and to families that may have stuck with conventional public education through graduation but been left with a sense that there must be something more. Almost every little college or university in the country is telling potential students that their indistinguishable institution is the path to a great career, an exciting social life, and self-fulfillment. Any college with the courage to offer students an opportunity to be part of something bigger than themselves will stand out.

Any college willing to stand for something more than instant gratification and stylish activism will distinguish itself like a thoroughbred in a field of donkeys. Leading with a statement like, "Every student at this university will leave it with a knowledge of Athens, the Federalist Papers, and the American constitution," might turn off the hordes looking for a place to drink and riot their way through four years of debauchery, but little colleges are already losing those students. Those are the students leaving anyway, to get the always cheaper, always easier education from regional state schools. The small college with the guts and faith to stand for something clear and particular will draw sufficient numbers seeking something more than run-of-the-mill training and thus will be able to sustain the college while institutions offering the same watered-down education, however much they speak of "excellence," will fail.

Many will come to these schools seeking a haven from the radical madness that reigns at American universities. That so many on today's college campuses don't want students to read Shakespeare or learn about Churchill might just inspire a small but significant number of prospective students to seek out those places still offering such topics. At the very least, students will be looking for places where they won't be required to take reeducation credits on the fluidity of gender or the ubiquity of empire.

When many American colleges seem too preoccupied with placating the Jacobins to bother with any actual education, sanity may be the best marketing strategy of all. That may be why the website for the University of Dallas proclaims that the school's "classical liberal arts education fosters the recovery and renewal of the Western intellectual tradition" and why the new honors college at the University of Tulsa promises its students that "by learning from great thinkers of the past, we prepare you for a life that is worth living." At least some colleges know that parents, and even many students, would like to find a school that doesn't condition its students to want to "eat the rich" or "smash the patriarchy," but rather to live a life shaped by virtue and wisdom.

Such a clear statement of values and commitments will not only draw students but will also draw donors. St. John's College, perhaps the best known of the "Great Books" liberal arts colleges, is betting on that. In 2019 St. John's cut tuition from $52,000 to $35,000. This reduction naturally increased applications, but the college is hoping that they will be able to make up the difference primarily through donations. Their fundraising efforts seem to be paying off. A university aiming, at best, to pass students along to high-paying jobs and, at worst, to indoctrinate students with a kind of lunacy rarely sustainable beyond campus is less likely to attract the generosity either of philanthropists or of small donors. A college that seeks to preserve the best in Western civilization and pass on a heritage of reason and virtue, however, may find itself in a stronger position for fundraising. Such colleges can offer more than a write-off; they can offer a cause. They provide the donor with a reason to give sacrificially.

Such robust and vocal traditionalism will require a great amount of courage on the part of administrations at small colleges. Conventional wisdom will tell them to follow the crowd, to ape the curriculum and values of the surrounding public institutions and elite private schools. But small, private colleges can no longer afford the blandness and mediocrity of massive, tax-subsidized public education. Nor can they coast on an elite past. They have to offer an alternative.

Just as a local mom and pop store will never compete with Walmart, much less with Amazon, by attempting to out-generalize the big guys, so too must the little college distinguish itself. And the clearest distinction comes in the ethos of the college. What does the school stand for? Is it possible to tell by looking at the college website and at various promotional materials that the school stands for anything in particular? If little colleges want to stay open, they should ask themselves if there is anything at stake regarding their continued existence beyond simply continuing to pay the faculty and field a football team.

Small colleges simply do not have the luxury of milquetoast commitments. For many years institutions of higher education were covered by the broad, vaguely Protestant consensus that determined the morality and culture in America. One assumed that the universities stood for the same broad consensus on values as other institutions in American life. But that broad consensus has broken down. In the resulting cultural chaos, it is a fantasy to think that a small college can be "above" the fray and coast by on bland commitments to "critical thinking" or career preparation. To attract students, the small liberal arts college will need to be vocal about what it stands for. Boldness is required for survival. Small colleges will need to fight against the current by doing things like revitalizing or resurrecting their classics departments and adding hours to their core while other universities are cutting back. It will be hard swimming upstream, but going with the flow is the path to oblivion.

The Fraud of Higher Education

IN *THE REPUBLIC*, Plato's Socrates tells of a man who lives with a beast. The beast is demanding, and the man must cater to its whims. Soon, the man becomes so accustomed to placating the beast that he comes to define what is good by what the beast wants, and what is bad by what the beast rejects. Plato ends this story by asking, "Does this man seem any different from the man who believes it is wisdom to have figured out the anger and pleasures—whether in painting, music, or particularly, in politics—of the multifarious many who assemble?"

In the field of education today, the beast is known as "consultants," "educational trends," or "best practices." Our colleges and universities now have vast appendages devoted solely to ministering to (the root meaning of *ad minister*) this beast of popular opinion. The result is an educational establishment that has abandoned the permanent things that give meaning and true sweetness to human life. Instead, our institutions of "higher learning" devote their energy and resources to chasing the flimsy trends of the moment.

Universities reduce or eliminate foreign language requirements to make sure that no "unnecessary" work stands between a student and his career-defined degree. They shrink the core curriculum (permitting pre-professional majors to inflate their share of credit hours) under the supposed pressure of maintaining accreditation from various professional societies—all so that their graduates can gain expertise in techniques and technologies that will be obsolete in a year or two. Perhaps worst of all, they replace the unified and coherent liberal arts core with a grab-bag of "gen-ed" requirements, so that the student who doesn't wish to read Cicero or Shakespeare can instead study soap operas or comic books and still call himself "educated." For regardless of what one has learned, it is the claim of having been to college—and the more name recognition for that college, the better—that earns one respect and a good job. It is in light of this decline in educational standards that we should understand the recent college admissions scandal, in which actors Felicity Huffman and Lori Loughlin, along with others, paid large amounts of money to get their children, through bribery and fraud, into "elite" universities.

If education is what the beast says it is, a mere means to the end of greater wealth and prestige, then what these parents did makes perfect sense. If the point is to possess credentials—not knowledge and wisdom—why wouldn't those with wealth use it to fake their children's credentials and accomplishments? Many of those outraged by the behavior of these celebrity parents share the foundational assumptions that make sense of such actions—that the point of education is not to "get wisdom," in the words of Proverbs, but to gain prestige. The parents who bribed their kids' way into college were just feeding the beast, the same as everybody else.

Universities are flailing and failing not despite their infatuation with the preoccupations of "the flies of a summer," but because of it. As many have noted, an alarming higher education bubble now exists, analogous to the housing bubble which burst in 2008. Never has the American consumer willingly paid so much hoping to get so little. Universities addicted to government-backed money are finding it harder to get their fix. As cheap alternatives to the multitudinous campuses offering mediocre education at premium prices pop up online or in storefronts around the country, the law of supply and demand kicks in. The watered-down, mediocre, and aimless college that can't survive on the life support of government funding is destined to die. The private university will have to get serious.

Private colleges that want to survive and even thrive must rediscover the pursuit of Truth, Goodness, and Beauty. Few "consultants" understand this, but devotion to the *summum bonum,* to a deeper understanding of human thriving, is the path to healthy academic institutions. It is also good business. The classical education movement in K–12 education is rapidly growing across the country, with many students and parents looking for a more meaningful form of education than the dreary factories we call public schools. Students who started kindergarten as the classical school movement began to pick up steam a decade ago are now looking for colleges that reflect and honor their intellectual values. The number of students seeking real education, focused on great books and the Western tradition, will continue to grow as more classical schools are founded each year. Astute colleges and universities are already courting these students by adding or expanding their offerings in classical languages and by creating great books programs. Meanwhile, other universities continue to feed the beast of popular opinion, which will eventually devour them when there are no more students to eat.

In a recent opinion piece for *The Chronicle of Higher Education,* Notre Dame sociologist Christian Smith called for a turn to "visionary traditionalism" as the best remedy for what ails higher education. In Smith's diagnosis, America's colleges are "drowning in B.S." He lists the abandonment of a belief in objective truth, the neglect of the liberal arts, the fragmentation of the core curriculum into ever-greater specialization, the one-sided political atmosphere on campuses, and the absurd coddling of students as among the contributing factors to this gruesome suffocation. As Smith recognizes, the best response to this state of affairs is not restless "innovation," or a chase after whatever "best practices" other mediocre universities have been pursuing for the last fifteen minutes. Only a "visionary traditionalism"—a bold return to long-standing educational principles in the West—can rid our universities of corrosive "B.S."

Visionary Traditionalism means a return to the great books and important ideas of the Western world. It means reviving classes in Hebrew, Greek, and Latin despite what consultants might say about the beast's demand for more pre-professional programs. Universities, especially private Christian universities, stay relevant not by chasing the needs of the moment, but by addressing themselves to the lasting questions in human life.

Part III

Poetry in the Age of Superficiality

IT IS TEMPTING to decry our age as the worst of times. Anyone who has studied history, however, knows that this complaint is unjust. For all our concern over gun violence, terrorism, and bullying, we pale in comparison to the violence of previous ages: no gladiatorial bloodbaths, very few Viking raids. There is the very real threat of mass violence inherent in our war technologies, but on the balance, daily life in the developed world is generally less violent than at any other point in history. If one is inclined to bewail the sexual immorality of our age, one might take a peek behind the curtain of antiquity. We've got nothing on the depravity of some of the Greeks and Romans, though we do seem to be warming up to make a run at matching them. Is our society unjust? Of course. Is it more just than all that have preceded it in the Western world? Obviously. Most Westerners today are freer, safer, and more prosperous than at any previous point in history. What we aren't is more thoughtful.

This is the age of superficiality.

I don't have room here to plumb the depths of our superficiality, but I will skim the surface to offer some indication of what I mean by "the age of superficiality." In *A Secular Age*, Charles Taylor points out how in modernity "[p]ursuing the goods of life and prosperity, while eschewing 'enthusiasm,' in a world designed especially to fa- vour these ends, seemed to make life shallow, devoid of deep resonance and meaning; it seemed to exclude transports of devotion, of self-giving, to deny a heroic dimension to our existence." Of course, many modern intellectual, artistic, and religious movements have developed to combat this feeling of superficiality. Yet the influence of these voices for depth has been waning in recent decades, drowned out by a popular culture that is quickly becoming our only culture.

Consider *Time* magazine and the online archive of its covers. In 1967, Robert Lowell was the last poet to appear on the cover of *Time*. He had been preceded by Robinson Jeffers, Gertrude Stein, Amy Lowell, Robert Frost, Carl Sandburg, T.S. Eliot, and Evgeny Evtushenko. Here are some people who have appeared on the cover since they last featured a poet: Leonardo DiCaprio (twice), Kanye West (twice), BB8, Darth Vader (four times, if you count young Anakin), Yoda, Spider-Man, Adele, Beyoncé, Taylor Swift, Angelina Jolie, Tom Hanks, Keanu Reeves, Russell Crowe, Bono (thrice), Tom Cruise (twice: with and without Nicole Kidman), Julia Roberts, Pikachu the Pokémon, Jerry Seinfeld, Jim Carrey, David Letterman, Jodie Foster, Bart Simpson, Kevin Costner, Superman, Mickey Mouse, Bette Midler, Molly Ringwald, the Alien from *Alien* and *Aliens*, Madonna, Crockett and Tubbs, Shirley MacLaine, Cheryl Tiegs (twice), Sylvester Stallone, Brooke Shields, Burt Reynolds, John Travolta, Warren Beatty, Diane Keaton, King Kong, Charlie's Angels, Cher, Elton John, Jaws, and Raquel Welch. To be fair, plenty of important political figures have appeared on the cover, but artists and intellectuals increasingly have not. As usual, novelists have fared *slightly* better than poets. Jonathan Franzen appeared on the cover in August of 2010; Mark Twain in July of 2008; Harry Potter (not J.K. Rowling) in June of 2003 and September of 1999; and Tom Wolfe in November of 1998. Norman Mailer was on the cover in 1973, but only in connection to Marilyn Monroe. Serious music has not done so well either, with nothing besides conductor James Levine in 1983 and Pavarotti in 1979.

My point is not that *Time* has not covered important stories. My point is about what kind of material has apparently fallen out of the category of important. Nor am I suggesting that *Time* is the voice of our age, just that it is a convenient marker for what Americans are thinking about. That Bill Gates and Steven Spielberg have been featured many times tells us that we think primarily about money and entertainment. Pop culture has become the only culture.

A widely discussed 2015 study by Andrew Powell-Morse showed that most pop songs are written at the third-grade reading level or below, steadily decreasing over the last ten years. Of course, pop music has always been pop music, but is there not a world of difference between Cole Porter, whose "Begin the Beguine" scores at about the eighth-grade reading level, and Maroon 5, whose hit songs average below the third-grade level? Sure, Porter is no Milton, but he does at least approach adulthood. The music that surrounds us is unlikely to provoke us to any emotion beyond the sentimental and saccharine on the one hand or juvenile angst on the other. It doesn't have the vocabulary to do anything more. Everyone knows that the Beatles appeared on *The Ed Sullivan Show* in 1964. What might be more surprising is that the great Israeli-American violinist Itzhak Perlman appeared on the same episode. Rock musicians continue to appear on late-night television, of course, but how many violinists do you see on screen with Jimmy Fallon, Seth Meyers, or Jimmy Kimmel these days? Our public fare is pure sugar. We are a nation with a mental junk-food problem.

Our morning network news programs typically give us about fifteen minutes of actual news followed by an hour or more of celebrity gossip and fluff. The most popular cable television shows offer little more than the pornography of violence and the violence of pornography. The once-lordly major networks have been given over almost entirely to the vapid wasteland of *The Bachelor* and *Big Brother*, vast stretches of nothingness that the average American can sit in front of for hours with no fear that our own empty lives will be made to seem cheap in light of some greater thoughtfulness or beauty. Our obsession with "Keeping up with the Kardashians" is a sure sign that we not only tolerate the vacuous and insipid but actually revere it.

My point is not that one might expect more from pop music or television (one might, but to insist seems futile); I mean, merely, to acknowledge the superficiality that is ubiquitous as mass culture drowns out all other forms of culture. It seems at times that smartphones and social media have expanded the dominion of pop culture into nearly every moment of our waking lives. It is now more than ever possible for Americans to live lives entirely untouched by anything that gestures toward transcendence.

Not too long ago in the grand scheme of history, a walk home in the evening might occasion some gazing at the stars, a situation in which even the most congenitally superficial person could eventually find himself pondering the meaning of it all. While few of us would come to very profound conclusions, we would at least be stretched in the exercise. No more. Thanks to our portable technology, one need never rise above the level of kitten videos, Tik-Tok dances, and what our friends are having for dinner. Despite the great potential the internet holds for enriching and expanding the public sphere, if we are honest we acknowledge that memes are a very different—a thinner, poorer—thing than ideas, for which they are substituted. As Sherry Turkle recounts in *Reclaiming Conversation*, studies show that the mere presence of a cell phone significantly reduces the chance of meaningful conversation. Our technology is pushing us toward lives of shallow consumerism and the sort of unceasing entertainment that rots our brains and withers our souls. Josef Pieper argued that leisure gives birth to culture. It is sadly ironic that it is now our zombie leisure, a debased thing lacking the dignity of the

Greek *scola* or the Roman *otium*, under which we are smothering the culture bequeathed to us.

Meanwhile, the pursuit of the True, the Good, and the Beautiful is, at best, tolerated. As the Marxist theorist Theodor Adorno puts it in "The Schema of Mass Culture,"

> from our earliest youth all of this [everything that is beautiful and good] is only admitted on the condition that it is not after all to be taken seriously. With every gesture the pupil is given to understand that what is most important is understanding the demands of "real life" and fitting oneself properly for the competitive realm, and that the ideals themselves were either to be taken as confirmation of this life or were to be immediately placed in its service.

It's fine to offer music classes or read a poem, as long as you can demonstrate how these things make students better at the "real" subjects we call STEM. But let's be sure to wink and sneer about their little choral groups or poetry clubs.

This superficiality is traceable in part to our abandonment of tradition. When we abandon tradition as a guiding element in life, far from liberating ourselves, we enslave ourselves to superficial convention. Rather than requiring unthinking allegiance, true tradition asks us to join in the thinking of the ages, to think along with Plato or Aquinas, as well as along with our parents and ancestors. Convention, however, asks us to accept whatever flimsy thing is given us at the moment, to share a meme or repeat a slogan. Convention has always played a strong part in daily life, but social media and mass culture have rapidly increased the prominence of convention in American life at a time in which local and national traditions are vanishing. Every aspect of our lives is increasingly temporary. Pop culture seems to cycle at an ever-faster rate. We might well ask how many of our own opinions are well-founded and measured against the wisdom of the ages and how many are merely fashionable. Tradition has depth, even to the point of usefully contradicting and correcting itself. Convention never fruitfully contradicts itself but is flat, flimsy, and brittle enough to easily break. Cut off from the depth of the tradition as embodied in great books, music, art, and ideas, as well as in organic local custom, we live in the shallows of mere convention.

What does poetry have to offer the men and women of such an age? The usual answers, mostly utilitarian in nature, are insufficient. Poetry in school will not improve students' job prospects or make them better office workers, but it is more important now than ever to teach poetry because poetry offers a unique antidote to the superficiality that dominates American culture.

Defenders of the humanities often declare that "employers want liberal arts graduates." Literary study is pitched as a way to build those "soft skills" that employers are supposedly eager to pay for, such as the ability to communicate well in writing, to read and follow directions, to relate empathetically to others, and perhaps to discuss things one actually knows very little about. Undeniably, literary study, including poetry, develops these skills. Nor do I doubt that employers desire these traits in their employees, though we optimistically overestimate how much (not a few employers are surely in the market for mindless corporate drones). But were those employers to change their minds about this preference, would we then abandon the liberal arts? The development of "soft skills" is inadequate as a rationale for the study of poetry because those who take this line aren't arguing at all for the value of literary studies; they are arguing for the value of programs in "soft-skills studies." Were the English departments to find more up-to-date methods for imparting those skills, then poetry would be out the window. If it were discovered that juggling and tightrope-walking develop these "soft skills" with twice as much accuracy and efficiency as studying poetry, wouldn't English professors be compelled to put away their Donne and their Frost to take up flaming knives and balance poles?

Even were English departments allowed to continue teaching poetry as a sort of second or third best way of developing "soft skills," they would be left teaching a discipline that has no inherent or internal order, only an external use. There would be no particular reason to teach Shakespeare or Dickinson if it were discovered that soft skills can be readily acquired by reading whatever is most popular on Instagram. Literary study would become everywhere what it is in too many places already: a discipline governed only by whim.

Further, no one goes to graduate school out of a passionate devotion to "soft skills," choosing a life teaching poetry due to a burning conviction that "those tech companies need people who can write well, and someone has to see that they get them!" It is a kind of bad faith to retroactively justify one's profession with something that has nothing to do with one's own attraction to it.

"Critical thinking," often listed among the "soft skills," is at least a little loftier goal than the writing of exceptionally clear office memos and is often evoked as nearly the single purpose for studying literature. Yet critical thinking also falls short for all of the same reasons that "soft skills" in general fail as a justification. Teaching students to think critically about ideas is indeed crucial—perhaps now more than ever, though I suppose thinkers have felt that way since at least Socrates—but it is far better accomplished by reading Plato's *Republic* or *The Federalist Papers* than by reading "The Song of Wandering Aengus." The English department justified by "critical thinking" can never be more than an ancillary to philosophy or political science and poetry itself nothing more than a randomly lineated exercise in obscuring thought only for the purpose of practice in untangling it. The "post-structuralist" approaches that in the last quarter of the twentieth century came to dominate literary study—with its emphasis on critical thinking and the exposure of power—have unfortunately bequeathed to professors of literature the utilitarian impulse to make literature merely a means to a political or social end. "Critical thinking"—or, as we might better call it, "*reason*"—should be left to the rhetoricians (with whom teachers of poetry often share a department and even a person) and to the philosophers. Learning to reason well is, no doubt, a critical component of a liberal arts education and of the study of the great books, but were it the only important justification, would we not then do well to follow Plato's most infamous suggestion and banish poets from our little republics of letters?

Well, then, could we not justify the teaching of poetry on the grounds that it leads to learning true justice? I think not, and for the same reasons I don't ascribe to the "soft skills" justification. Poetry almost certainly is not now—and definitely could not remain—the best, or even one of the top ten—ways to learn about justice. Here, again, I think the teacher of poetry would be much wiser to yield the floor to colleagues in philosophy, history, and politics. Or rather the teacher of letters must know when one is teaching the history of thought and when one is teaching poetry *qua* poetry. No doubt the reading of some poems—*Paradise Lost, The Divine Comedy,* Claudia Rankine's *Citizen*—can lead us into contemplation of justice, and no doubt we will thus find ourselves at times discussing justice in the course of discussing poetry. The same, however, could be said of agriculture or jazz. Justice is just one of many important topics addressed in poetry and thus hardly adequate to justify the whole endeavor.

Those who see in poetry a means of learning justice, however, often have in mind not the gleaning of insights from sage poets but rather the use of poetry as a negative example. This tendency to focus on the negative ideological aspects of the poet is greater the further back one goes in the curriculum. It is typical to focus on the heroes in contemporary literature but to find mainly villains in the "Survey of British Literature" course. We learn justice, many educators seem to think, by tearing through the canon to see how unjust poets of the past were and how marred by injustice their monuments remain. If a particular poem, however, offers nothing more than a record of wrong thinking, isn't it better consigned to oblivion? Of course, we note the moral flaws in the poems we read; it is impossible to teach Spenser's *Faerie Queene* well without noting that he was monstrously unjust toward the Irish, as C.S. Lewis said. But were that lack of justice the whole point why bother to teach Spenser at all? If one cannot see the beauty in Spenser's lushly imaginative epic, he would be better off forgotten, as he no doubt soon would be without English professors to prop him up. It is possible to note frankly and directly that Ezra Pound's politics were abominable and then move on to discuss more substantially the beauty and economy of the language with which he engages Homer in the opening passages of the *Cantos*. If the point one is making is simply that Ezra Pound was a fascist, why bother with the *Cantos* at all? Indeed, why bother with Pound? If one wishes to illustrate the evils of fascism, there are surely more important cases to discuss. Pound is a major poet; as a player in twentieth-century politics, he is below the minor league.

Rejecting these various utilitarian rationales for teaching poetry does not mean we must fall back into an anemic "art for art's sake" position. Poetry does some good in the world. This good is, however, more nuanced than "soft skills" or "critical thinking" or "justice," as fine and important as those things certainly are. Teaching poetry is not disconnected from a formative education that takes virtue as its goal.

The teaching of poetry matters greatly in the age of superficiality, because poetry uniquely and especially calls us back to tradition and to traditional use of symbol. It calls us out of the shallows into the deeper water of human experience. It draws us toward transcendence. And acknowledging transcendence is a first step, and a constant walk, in any sane and virtuous life.

In arguing for poetry's ability to take us beyond mere convention and into contact with a great tradition, I am arguing for the importance of the canon. I'm not, at the moment, arguing for any particular iteration of the canon but rather merely for the concept of "canonical literature." Great poetry makes a great chain of time, and to read poems in the context of a canon calls us out from the chronological provincialism that stunts our hearts, minds, and souls. We should conceive of the canon not as a fixed list of dead authors, but as a living, breathing presence, an ongoing election that has lasted generations, a working thesis. The student who travels the road back from Blake to Milton, from Milton to Dante, from Dante to Virgil, from Virgil to Homer has traveled far beyond the momentary yet infinitely repeating confines of popular culture: the number one movie, the number one song, this week and every week unto the crack of doom. The road to Homer is, of course, just one road through a vast country. The canonical country has borders, but those borders remain porous. The very act of maintaining the canon—of pondering what has been in, what should no longer be left out—cultivates a sense of the spaciousness of time.

All good poetry participates in tradition. Poetry by its nature is allusive, even when the allusion is embedded in form rather than content. Even avant-garde work draws its energy from violation of a tradition the reader is expected to know. A Shakespearean sonnet and Tzara's "cut up poems" both work from a concept of what poetry is, or at least participate in the question of "what is poetry?" In that, they share equally in a sense of the canonical.

Poetry also frees us from convention through its preoccupation

with classical topoi, by which I mean not stale rhetorical exercises but
rather powerful currents of thought and feeling running deeper than
mere convention. We might gesture toward them with fragments of
Latin—*carpe diem, ubi sunt, memento mori*—but they are not reducible
to catchphrase. Consider, for example, the picture of life lived simply
and well as it has been embodied in poems throughout the last two
thousand years, from Horace's second epode, which begins, "Happy
is that man who, far from business cares, / like the ancient human
race, / works his father's land with his ox," to Martial's epigram 10:47
as loosely translated by Henry Howard, the Earl of Surrey:

> Martial, the things for to attain
> The happy life be these, I find:
> The riches left, not got with pain;
> The fruitful ground, the quiet mind. . . .

Already in these brief few lines we can sense something deeper than
the merely contemporary calling to us.

    We might consider how the *topos* is picked up by Yeats in his "The
Lake Isle of Innisfree":

> I will arise and go now, and go to Innisfree,
>   And a small cabin build there, of clay and wattles made:
> Nine bean-rows will I have there, a hive for the honey-bee;
> And live alone in the bee-loud glade.

From there, we might turn to certain poems by Frost or by Jane
Kenyon, and while there is no plain straight line between Horace's
rural laborer and Frost's or Kenyon's New Englanders, we sense in
these poems a similar invitation to ponder, to dwell on, a certain,
though undefined, aspect of human experience. Reading these po-

ems we come to know things we must feel and see our way toward, things we could not really be told directly. The *topoi* are encountered incarnated in great poetry. They are not simple "morals of the story" but rather places where beauty meets truth in subtle and various ways within the physical world we all inhabit.

As the traditionalist and the deconstructionist can agree, poetry breaks down our sense of easy one-to-one correspondence. Poetry gestures toward a state of true allegory. In the age of Dante, Western thought saw the cosmos as richly significant, a book written by God in which every detail gestured beyond itself: If a clover had three leaves, it was to gesture toward the Trinity, and if it had four leaves, it was to point us to the four gospels. Despite all the good done by the scientific revolution, we can't deny that it in some ways impoverished us in changing the Western world's dominant metaphor for the cosmos from a book to a machine. We gained an ability to deal with nature in wonderful ways—for all my love of the past, I would not wish to return to a world without penicillin, or even air-conditioning—but with Newton's new and mechanistic universe we began a slow decline from symbol into sign. I think we have now reached the bottom. We look at the world and see no deep signification. If this is a result of what Charles Taylor calls the "disenchantment" of the modern world, it is aided and abetted by our addiction to superficial mass culture. But poetry can help. As Billy Collins says in "Poetry, Pleasure, and the Hedonist Reader," "[t]he philosophical motive behind poetic comparisons is, then, to move the world closer to the condition of harmony, ultimately an absolute harmony in which all things are connected, a simile-and-metaphor-riddled world where everything is like everything else." Poetry gives us our depth perception back.

Teachers of poetry, then, must cease their complicity in the eclipse and diminishment of their own object of study and reclaim the core curriculum rather than petitioning for a few extra moments given to

Keats or Eliot if there is extra time after all the important STEM and professional subjects. To do so will require using embarrassing words like "soul" and "beauty" and insisting that there are few things in life more important. The job of the true educator, more than preparing students for their job, is to prepare students for the possibility of unemployment, to give them the resources of soul to see life as more than a means to a paycheck and to sit in their own company through the long night of doubt. Only true education can hold back the rising tide of the overwhelming shallows.

Why Local Poetry Matters

I HAVE FRIENDS who are into the "local food" movement, refusing to eat anything not grown within a small radius of their home. I have other, and some of the same, friends who are into local music, rejecting the corporate world of big labels in favor of bands they can follow at local clubs. I used to know one person who "dresses local," refusing to use any material in her clothing not generated within a short journey from her home. Local is the big thing now, and with good reason. I wonder, however, if in this rush to embrace our inner Wendell Berry we haven't overlooked one very important category of the local: the local poet. I think it is often assumed that "local poetry" is amateur poetry, and only the poet of national reputation matters. This certainly seems to be the attitude of most MFA programs, which, with a few notable exceptions, rarely encourage their students or faculty to get involved in the coffee house readings, critique groups, or small journals and presses of local poetry scenes. So let me outline some of the reasons why local poetry is worth investing one's time, and even one's money, in.

All good poetry is rooted in some particular place, and a local poetry scene helps to keep poetry rooted and particular. Think about how much television has done to flatten out the rich variety of American dialects and accents. If we think of American literature as only significant on the national level, then we are in danger of flattening out the rich variety of American poems, reaching only for some nationally acceptable standard: the flat non-accent of the nightly news anchor. Honestly, I sometimes think we are already on the verge of a literary culture in which every poem takes place in some unidentifiable and uniform suburbia or hip urban neighborhood. A thriving local poetry scene encourages a poetry of particular place, images and topics grounded in the shared experience of the local audience. Rather than creating an insular poetry, this opens up avenues to the universal through the particular. Think of Robert Frost's or Jane Kenyon's New England or Christian Wiman's Texas. Like food, poetry that seems substantial, that seems real and nourishing, comes from someplace identifiable. The poetry that best embodies real experience and real particulars is not produced purely for export. It speaks into a place first and then through it to the wider world.

If local poets in the smaller places of this country aren't so focused on exporting their poems, they are free to focus on building literary community where they are. Local poetry scenes provide a support group for practicing poets. For poets who have graduated from MFA programs, the local scene can be a place to continue the camaraderie and support they have come to rely upon. Perhaps more importantly, the local scene provides encouragement, support, and feedback for poets who are outside the MFA system for cultural, financial, or other reasons. Long before the rise of the Iowa workshops, developing writers were nourished by rich local scenes: Ben Jonson and associates gathered at the Mermaid tavern, and twentieth-century American expats congregated in the cafes of Paris. It is only the success that time has brought such local coalitions which keeps us from thinking of these writers as "local."

I might add that it is in these local communities, and certainly not in the academy, that the great developments in poetics have taken place. In reading David Lehman's account of the "New York School of Poets," *The Last Avant-Garde,* I was struck by just how local these poets were. Ashbery, O'Hara, Schuyler, and Koch may be very cosmopolitan in their outlook, but it was their proximity to each other (with the exception of Ashbery's time in France), their appearances at the same parties and the same bars, the same galleries and the same readings, that gave them the opportunity to develop together approaches arguably needed to freshen up American poetry at mid-century. One may counter that these sorts of incubating communities can now occur nationally via the internet or through the gathering of prominent poets onto campuses, but I would argue that internet versions—unlike the communal life, the shared experience— are always more plastic and contrived, more about abstract ideas than about literary passions and tend to fizzle out quickly, fossilized forever on abandoned websites. As for the campus as a place for new poetics to emerge through creative community, one might point out that such artistic cross-fertilization is often nipped in the bud by the alarming vagrancy, the nomadic spirit, of the typical creative-writing faculty. When it isn't, when one finds a core group of writers working side by side on a campus year after year, then what one has is, in fact, simply a very solid, relatively well-paid version of the local poetry scene, at its best often interacting with local poets off campus as well. Sadly, though, even poets long established at a particular university can focus all their literary energies at the "national level," neglecting the literary world just past the edges of the campus, especially if they happen to be located somewhere outside the traditional centers of literary activity on the east coast. But when local poets interact, on campus and off, one gets the variety of influences and pressures, of poetics and approaches, that fosters creativity. Contrary to what snobbery would dictate, poets grouped nationally are much more isolated aesthetically than the poets at the local coffee shop reading, where one might hear a language poet reciting a string of punctuation marks one minute and a neo-confessional poet detailing his latest breakup or breakdown the next, and, after that, maybe even a Shakespearean sonnet.

Perhaps less obviously, the local poetry scene gives poets a chance to define artistic and career success in terms that are both more realistic and more meaningful. According to an article Seth Abramson wrote for the *Huffington Post*, there are forty-five thousand poets graduating from MFA programs every decade and twenty thousand books of poetry published every ten years in the US. If, as Ecclesiastes put it, "there is no end to the making of books," then the deciding factor on who "makes it big" and who doesn't—out of the pool of the thousands of most talented, ambitious, and determined poets—is more often than not simple luck. The smaller, local poetry community, however, provides an arena in which a poet can build a meaningful reputation based more on accomplishment than luck or connection. Before you dismiss this notion as simply settling for the minor leagues, consider that when Shakespeare, Jonson, and Donne were building their great reputations during the Renaissance, the combined population of England and Wales was about four million, which is not significantly more than the current population of Oklahoma. London, the real home of literary reputation in the age of Shakespeare, was itself significantly less populated than Oklahoma City today. Dante made his great reputation as the national poet of a country a good bit smaller than the state of California. If you figure in the lower rates of literacy in the past, it becomes even more apparent that a contemporary American writer aiming for national importance is up against numbers unfathomable in any precursor literary community. A local poetry scene, with established readings, journals, and presses, gives a poet a more reasonable measure of success. There is great honor in being one of the best of where you are, wherever that may be.

We've recently gone through another perennial round of hand-wringing over the supposedly dwindling audience for poetry, the ever-present "Can Poetry Matter?" debate. In that *Huffington Post* article Abramson posted a list of two hundred "national figures" who will make you care about poetry. As much as I admire the people on the list, and as grateful as I am for their large-scale investment in the art of poetry, I couldn't help thinking that local poets can do a heck of a lot more than any "national figure" to revive the public's appetite for the art of poetry. The uninitiated into the marvels of poetry are much more likely to wander into a coffee shop reading than into a large lecture hall to hear a national poet. Local poetry can spread a love for the art from person to person, neighbor to neighbor, at the "grassroots" level. This is why states have poets laureate.

So if you care about poetry at all, support your local poets. Go to readings (you could even host a house-reading at your place). Buy books. Subscribe to the journals that live where you live. You don't have to stop paying attention to the big, nationally known poets. Just try to save some of your support and encouragement for the poet whose kid goes to school with yours, or who sits in the pew behind you at church, or who teaches at your local community college. And if you are a local poet, wear the mantle proudly.

Six Poets for People Who Think They Don't Like Poetry

THE BEST COMPLIMENT I ever received came with chocolate pie. For a museum fundraiser, I was asked to read after a pie auction. Afterwards, I was enjoying a hard-earned slice of French silk when a man walked up and said, "Ever since high school, I thought I didn't like poetry. I was here for the pie. But I liked your poems. I could identify with them. Maybe I was wrong about poetry." Best compliment ever.

A lot of well-meaning teachers spoil poetry for their students by presenting poems as a secret code to be cracked. A good poem, however, is not a puzzle. It is a pleasure. A poem may be wonderfully mysterious, but it should never be simply baffling. A poem may invite us to read more, and even send us to other books to learn more in order to more fully enter its world. It shouldn't, however, simply turn us away.

Yet generations of students have been taught that poems hate us, that they want to confuse and even shame us. And so generations of students have turned away from poetry. When is the last time you saw someone on a bus or a plane reading a volume of poems?

All is not lost. There are poets who offer a way back in, poets whose poems offer the pleasures of good verse. For the poetry-averse, I recommend the following six poets. These poets represent a great variety of techniques and perspectives, so if you don't like one, try another.

Jane Kenyon

An American poet active from the late seventies to the early nineties, Jane Kenyon is often remembered for her compelling life story. Born in the Midwest, she fell in love with one of her professors at the University of Michigan, the renowned poet Donald Hall, married, and moved with him to his family farm in New England to devote their lives to writing poems. This romantic idyll was cut tragically short when Kenyon died in 1995, leaving behind just four complete books of poetry and a posthumous edition of "new and selected" poems called *Otherwise*.

Kenyon's work appeals through an exquisite combination of plain style and spiritual depth. Her poems are both understated and frank, like a conversation with a friend who is wise and sensible, unflinching and yet consoling. In "Father and Son," she hears her neighbors cutting wood and imagines the father "stepping back from the logs and aromatic / dust, while his son kicked the billets / down the sloping drive toward the shed." This is a moment of quiet connection, a simple and true-to-life picture of two men quietly at work together. When we learn, at the poem's end, that the wood will be used to warm the father and son through their last winter together, we are already comforted by the unstated yet apparent love between them and by the quiet dignity of their labor. One of her best-known poems, "Let Evening Come," seems, at least in retrospect, to offer the same kind of preparation for her own death. "Let the light of late afternoon / shine through chinks in the barn, moving / up the bales as the sun moves down," she writes, knowing

how great a consolation is beauty even as one must move into the
"late afternoon" of a life.

Her poems can also be quirky, even funny. In "Changes," she describes the move to the farm and how the sensible, rural New England
neighbors must view this pair of poets as completely impractical,
as foolish as the local boy who "used to chase cars / and bicycles,
howling, / waving his arms in the air." When reading her "Church
Fair" many of us can chuckle with recognition at this portrait of her
grandmother: "'Mrs. Kenyon,' the doctor used to tell her, / 'you are
simply killing yourself with work.' / This she repeated often, with
keen satisfaction." "Keen" would also be the best way to describe Jane
Kenyon as an observer of life.

B.H. Fairchild

Born in Texas and raised around the oil fields of Kansas, Oklahoma,
and Texas, B.H. Fairchild writes about the hardscrabble lives of
working men and women, often finding dignity, even holiness, in
the lives of people others might consider "losers."

In an age when many contemporary poets are fixated on fragmentation and nonlinear thinking, Fairchild has remained dedicated to
narrative. His recent *The Blue Buick: New and Selected Poems* offers
poems that read like exceptionally trim short stories. In one of his
best-known poems, "Body and Soul," he tells the story of a young
Mickey Mantle playing as a ringer in an amateur game. The poet
focuses not on the gifted young player, however, but on the old men
sitting around remembering the day they met him, the day they
discovered "the vast gap between talent and genius." This is a story
about ordinary men marked by their encounter with greatness.

Fairchild's poems often tell stories of desperation and transcendence among hardworking people on the plains. In "Rave On," he depicts four high school boys so hungry for meaning and a sense of being alive that they spend their evenings repairing junk cars solely for the excitement of intentionally wrecking them. In "Beauty," he confesses that "no male member of my family has ever used / this word in my hearing or anyone else's except / in reference, perhaps, to a new pickup or dead deer." And yet the story he tells is of men desperate for some glimpse of beauty, even as they are shamed by the light it casts on their dim lives. No one has written better about rural masculinity.

Marilyn Nelson

Marilyn Nelson is one of several poets associated with the "New Formalists," a group of poets rising to prominence in the '80s and '90s with a goal of returning poetry to rhyme, meter, and narrative in order to bring an audience back. Many of its main proponents appeared in the 1995 anthology *Rebel Angels: 25 Poets of the New Formalism*. Her poems—often focused on family and the African-American experience—are accessible yet rich with mystery.

Nelson's poems are hospitable to the reader—they don't resist being read, as so many contemporary poems seem to—yet she is not afraid to address harrowing subject matter. Her volume of new and selected poems, *The Fields of Praise*, offers many examples of her best work as she writes with sympathy and humanity about the massacres between the Hutu and Tutsi as well as about tragedies closer to her home. In "April Rape," the poet vividly and sympathetically imagines the inner life of a rape survivor who has barricaded herself in so that "the mouths of all the locks in the house / snatch at her like cats." The poem is a testimony of survival. Other poems, like

"No, No, Bad Daddy" and "Woman Kills and Eats own Infant," look unflinchingly at the human capacity for evil and the potential for human relationships to go horribly wrong. Yet these poems are not lurid or despairing. They offer a sense of shared sorrow and thus a sense of common humanity. Nelson's poems remind us again and again that we don't belong only to ourselves. Her poems of family and community explore the nets of love and obligation—the shared joys and burdens—that tie us together.

Andrew Hudgins

Andrew Hudgins, another veteran of the *Rebel Angels* anthology, is very much a Southern poet, and like many Southerners, he knows how to tell a good story. His 1985 debut collection, *Saints and Strangers*, includes a sequence of poems narrated by the daughter of a revivalist preacher. The sequence is like a novella in verse, following the main character through her childhood into adulthood and a family of her own. His second book, *After the Lost War*, is a fictionalized account of the life of Georgia poet, Sidney Lanier, who was a Confederate soldier before becoming a musician, writer, and professor.

Even when Hudgins's poems aren't narratives, they maintain a straightforward, conversational manner. One of his best poems, "The Hereafter," amusingly mulls over various possible versions of life after death before confessing that he has long pictured humans as the nails "God drives into the oak floor of this world," a conception of life that makes it "hard to comprehend the hammer turned / to claw me out." Has anyone ever written as vividly about the human inability to face our mortality?

Hudgins titled his 2013 memoir *The Joker*, and his most recent book of verse is *A Clown at Midnight*, so it is no surprise that comedy abounds in his volume of new and selected poems, *American Rendering*. In "Praying Drunk," he begins "Our Father who art in heaven, I am drunk. / Again." In that line break one discerns the knack for comic timing crucial in a good conversationalist or storyteller. "Playing Dead" recounts how his father used to lie perfectly still and let the children poke him until they were convinced that he was dead. The poem's young protagonist begins to fear the worst, introducing the element of anxiety found in most great comedy, until he tries jabbing his father in "the family jewels," a move that brings a quick end to the game.

Du Fu

While the rest of the poets on this list are contemporary and American, I want to include one poet who is not. Living from AD 712 to 770, in Tang Dynasty China, Du Fu attempted and failed to make a life as a civil servant. In an age marred by rebellions and civil unrest, he struggled to care for his family while writing hundreds of beautiful poems.

Du Fu speaks to us in ways that seem contemporary. Like Marilyn Nelson, he reminds us of our interdependence. In one of his most anthologized poems, the poet is reunited with his family after a brief separation in the turmoil. As the family embraces, the neighbors all peer over the garden wall and weep with joy. Few poets have so vividly and succinctly captured what it means to live a private life within the context of a community.

Friendship is a frequent theme in Du Fu's work. In a heart-wrenching poem about fleeing with his family from the rebels overrunning their village, he writes with palpable gratitude about the friend who took them in when they were on the verge of starvation, bathed their feet, and brought them platters of food. Elsewhere he writes of friends met on the road and of friends who have passed from this life. Again and again, his poems call us to meditate on our connections to other people.

Du Fu is also a precise observer of nature, often weaving natural images into his depictions of everyday life. In the homecoming poem mentioned above, for instance, he tells us that a sparrow sits and chirps on the gate as the poet comes home. The detail contributes not only by filling out the picture but also by subtly reminding the reader of the contrast between the seemingly eternal stability of nature and the changeableness of human fortunes.

There are many fine translations of Du Fu's work, but I recommend David Young's *Du Fu: A Life in Poetry* as a starting place. Young has translated the Tang poet's work into straightforward and accessible verse, and he has arranged the poems to tell the life story of the poet. It is a book I cherish and carry with me often.

Aaron Belz

Compared to the rest of the poets on this list, Aaron Belz is a young upstart, but he has proven himself to be a poet with great appeal to a general reading audience. Like Hudgins, Belz is a joker. Consider just a few titles of Belz's poems: "2005 Is an Important Year for Alec Baldwin," "Thomas Hardy the Tank Engine," and "Arguing with a Buddhist."

Belz is a master of silly word play. In "Hippie Slang," he tells us that, when he says he "digs" graves, he means "I enjoy and/or / understand them." In another poem, he imagines people in the horse-drawn carriage rental business "at loggerheads" with the inventors of the typewriter over who owns the phrase "carriage return."

Belz often mocks literature itself. In "Michael Jashbery," he mashes John Ashbery—author of the Pulitzer Prize–winning *Self-Portrait in a Convex Mirror*—with Michael Jackson, to get "I'm starting with the man / in the convex mirror." In another poem, he reduces Robert Browning's famous dramatic monologue "My Last Duchess" to "She was too flirtatious so I had her killed. / Now I want to marry your master's daughter." The great modernist poet, Marianne Moore, famously begins her poem, "Poetry," with the confession, "I, too, dislike it." If you have felt the same, reading Aaron Belz's irreverent romp through literary culture can be a therapeutic form of revenge.

Maybe reading these poets will convince you to dislike poetry a little less. Maybe they will be a gateway to the many great poets not included in this list. If you want more recommendations, I'd be happy to give you a thousand names.

Reticence and Expansiveness in Oklahoma Poetry

NOW IS A GOOD TIME to be an Oklahoman writer. We live and work in an Oklahoman Renaissance. In part, developments in higher education, like the addition of undergraduate and graduate writing programs throughout the state and the talent they attract and nurture, explain this sudden confluence of accomplished writers. But there is a deeper reason. Oklahoma is ripe for renaissance after the past century and more of suffering. Sorrows artistically fertilize a place. After the Wars of Roses and then the religious controversies and two-way martyrdom in England, Shakespeare, Spenser, Jonson, and Donne wrote masterpieces. Out of the renewed struggles of twentieth-century Ireland Yeats, Synge, and Heaney shaped poetry and drama. Harlem gave us the songs of Langston Hughes and Countee Cullen. Oklahoma has seen bloodshed and injustice in the conflict between white settlers and Native cultures. We've seen the struggle of the pioneer in an inhospitable climate, the Dust Bowl, the Murrah bombing, tornado after tornado, and drought. Oklahomans know hard times. This suffering bears fruit in the novels of Rilla Askew and in the poems of Jim Barnes. Though the weight of this suffering may be expressed directly in poems and stories about what Oklahoma has been through, it need not be expressed directly to be present. Oklahoma writers offer an abundance of subject matter grounded in suffering, but whatever the topic, they display a quality developed through suffering and its inheritance, a quality which I can only call *soulfulness.*

One of the most convincing treatises on aesthetics I have ever read is James Baldwin's short story "Sonny's Blues." Baldwin tells the story of a straitlaced teacher, the narrator of the story, who seems to think he has escaped being defined by suffering, until his reunion with his troubled musician brother, Sonny. At the story's climax the narrator has an unparaphrasable epiphany while listening to Sonny play piano with his jazz combo:

> He and his boys up there were keeping it new, at the risk of ruin, destruction, madness, and death, in order to find new ways to make us listen. For, while the tale of how we suffer, and how we are delighted, and how we may triumph is never new, it always must be heard. There isn't any other tale to tell, it's the only light we've got in all this darkness. . . . He had made it his: that long line, of which we knew only Mama and Daddy. And he was giving it back, as everything must be given back, so that, passing through death, it can live forever. I saw my mother's face again, and felt, for the first time, how the stones of the road she had walked on must have bruised her feet. I saw the moonlit road where my father's brother died. And it brought something else back to me, and carried me past it. I saw my little girl again and felt Isabel's tears again, and I felt my own tears begin to rise.

That "making it his" is an individual process, but it can be a cultural process also: the narrator also speaks of "with what burning we had yet to make it ours." This artistic/cultural process of building from ash is enlivening the literary arts in Oklahoma, something like what Auden must have meant when he said of Yeats: "Mad Ireland hurt you into poetry." Two prominent aspects of the Oklahoma experience deepen this process of artistic fertilization: reticence and expansiveness.

Reticence is one of the most important tools in the poet's toolbox. It is perhaps crucial to all really great poetry. Even in Walt Whitman's sprawling "Song of Myself" there is a great amount that is crucially left unsaid, a lot that Whitman has the wisdom to know is unsayable. These gaps give the poem much of its grandeur. A poem should be able to gesture beyond itself, shouldn't suggest that its own words cover all there is to say on a subject.

I grew up surrounded by people who know when to talk and when to shut up, what to say and what is better said when left unsaid. These were also storytelling people, but this is not a contradiction: the power of their stories depended greatly on what was left unsaid. These were not people who needed "mission statements" or "clearly defined objectives." They knew what needed doing and did it. They knew what was important and prioritized it in action. When they spoke, it meant something.

Nathan Brown, my predecessor as poet laureate, knows how to resist verbosity. His book *Less is More, More or Less* is an extended experiment with artistic reticence, consisting entirely of poems that would fit on standard-sized index cards. Rarely is a poet so considerate of other people's time. Brown's self-imposed discipline results in poems that aren't less complete, but rather somehow more fully realized in the silence that surrounds them. Here, for instance, is the poem "Tool":

I heard
this morning
    somewhere
    out my window

    a meticulous raven
  tapping out his memoir
on a fence pipe
with a nail.

This tiny poem says a lot about art, about the urge to sing, about the artist's use of the tools at hand, but it says all of this by not saying it, by simply letting the image resonate. Beginning poets have difficulty learning this discipline and restraint, but a life lived among plain-spoken Okies of few words is a good head start.

Ken Hada, a professor at East Central University and a quintessentially Oklahoman poet, has mastered the art of reticence. I often offer his poem "Dad's Sled" as a model for students when trying to instill a sense of restraint. The poem opens not with philosophical statement, sweeping setting, or any kind of emotional context but simply with the materials out of which the sled is constructed—exactly the detail that would have been first conveyed by any of my taciturn relatives: "He built it with used two by fours / scrap metal for runners. / He always saved spare parts." This opening economically introduces the character of the father with detail suggestive of his life experiences and personality, yet it states nothing overtly beyond a simple, common habit. The next stanza gives us his succinct explanation for his habit, "We might use that someday," which in few words suggests a hard-worn people's assumptions about what the future holds, about the necessity to be prepared for lean times. The poet's own response of "sure enough" echoes the father's wisdom without belaboring the point. The rest of the poem conveys vividly and sparingly a memory of a specific snowy day before the final stanza makes its philosophical point: "his ability to make happiness / out of things left over, used / and otherwise abandoned." The reader knows something is being said here about family, about class, about identity, yet nothing of the sort is said outright at all. The point is all the more powerful for its silence, as the poet gives the point room to bloom in the reader's mind.

Ron Wallace's "Learning to Speak Choctaw" is another small masterpiece of reticence. The poem begins with focused imagery and tightly observed detail:

> He rose like smoke from high grass
> and weeds that had taken the alley
> east of the Katy tracks
> and shuffled across the gravel road
> black hair, black eyes,
> a hundred creases in a dark brown face.

The rest of the poem unfolds from the small talk of two Choctaw adults: the out-of-work veteran named Earl and the poet's policeman father. The conversation reveals much while saying little: "'Hello, Earl, / I'm fine. Need a ride to town?' / 'Jus' walking, Captain.'" Earl asks to borrow some change for a hamburger. The elder Wallace provides the coin without commentary, and Earl succinctly replies, "Yokoke, my policeman friend. / I owe you four quarters now; I know." This simple exchange implies much about community, hard times, loss, and resilience. The final stanza is the poem's greatest example of effective reticence:

"War and wine,
    goddamned war and wine,"
        Dad melted back
    into the Chevy's engine;
    "Throw the ball, Son,
        just keep throwin' the ball."

This limited commentary and refusal to say more is a restrained but powerful summation not only of the tragedy of Earl's life but also of the commonplace nature of the tragedy. This is as Homeric a stroke as one sees in contemporary poetry, and it enacts its subject, reticence in the face of the unspeakable, in its poetic strategies, packing much into the father's entreaty to "just keep throwin' the ball."

Such powerful reticence also graces the work of Oklahoma native Quraysh Ali Lansana. Here is the entirety of his poem "Bible Belted: Communion":

did not know
black folks could be
catholic until I moved
to chicago. i was twenty-five.

This poem creates resonance by saying very little. Lansana gives the insight plenty of room to bloom for the reader, making the white space around the small poem an important part of its overall effect. The conceptual work of the poem happens in that empty space. A reticent man's greatest virtue is that he gives others room to think. The lack of capitalization and the poet's restraint—he could have easily tried to make a bigger splash by giving "i was twenty-five" it's own line—add to the effect of powerful understatement. Lansana says a lot about culture and acculturation, home, naiveté, expectations, and he does so with impressive economy. More than just a quality in the verse, reticence is the primary poetic strategy in this and many of Lansana's poems.

Perhaps I've said too much about reticence.

Expansiveness also characterizes the best Oklahoman poetry. Expansiveness seems like the opposite of reticence, a muchness in contrast to an absence. Think, however, of the Southern Plains that cover so much of Oklahoma, and you will begin to envision a landscape that epitomizes the union of muchness and absence, of reticence and expansiveness. Rich poetic expansiveness can be a direct result of the landscape. A strict rationalist might object to the proposition that landscape can so affect character, but think of Plato's discussion of music in *The Republic*, where in discussing the education of children, he very convincingly outlines the ability of different kinds of music to shape and mold our souls. Raise your child on Mozart or raise your child on Metallica: the choice surely influences the formation of the child's character. If one form of aesthetic experience can so obviously shape us, is it really so hard to believe that the constant aesthetic input of our natural surroundings can have a significant effect on our identities, our minds, and our souls?

Poetic expansiveness, as I mean it, is a "rejection of closure," in the words of the avant-garde poet Lyn Hejinian, though I don't mean to imply that it is a quality only of experimental poetry. I'm not talking about length or epic scope in subject matter. Rather, I mean a kind of openness, a breadth of spirit, a "don't fence me in" approach to writing. This quality is hard to pin down exactly, but is exemplified in the work of Joy Harjo, one of Oklahoma's best-known poets—for example, in her poem "Remember":

> Remember the sky that you were born under,
> know each of the star's stories.

Remember the moon, know who she is.
Remember the sun's birth at dawn, that is the
strongest point of time. Remember sundown
and the giving away to night.

While some poems may be described as creating "the sound of a
box clicking shut"—as Yeats had it—this poem in its entirety is an
exercise in opening up, in erasing boundary lines the way hard lines
of division—even those between earth and sky—are erased when
seen from the great distances of the plains.

Sometimes this expansiveness takes the form of longing, as anyone
who has stood alone looking into wide-open spaces and felt a sublime
longing knows. One of Oklahoma's great literary impresarios, Jeanetta
Calhoun Mish—who runs Mongrel Empire Press—expresses this
longing in a poem from her first collection, *Work Is Love Made Visible*.
The poem "To Ask and Be Answered" addresses Walt Whitman
(the master of American expansiveness) and evokes Allen Ginsberg
as well as Emily Dickinson. The poem is confident in its voice but
clearly open to other voices as well, personal yet communal in a way
that we saw in Joy Harjo's poem. Here is the ending of the poem:

I am thinking of Walt Whitman
because there is a certain slant of sorrow in my heart
that has transformed everything;
because I am aching to be expansive,
to embrace the world as it is,
because I believe that loving the world
in its wholeness might save me from melancholy,
because I am convinced that in the refuge of
his wisdom I will find equanimity
because I am desperate for a reaching 'round of his lyrical arms,

desiring to imagine myself sacred in his eyes,
longing to ask and to be answered in affirmation,

are you thinking of me, Walt Whitman?

The repetition of "because" at the beginning of the line—a rhetorical device associated with Whitman, and later Ginsberg, and known as *anaphora*—runs throughout the poem and adds to the feeling of openness, of expansiveness, by suggesting a multiplicity of causes behind the poet's longing. It is an open and expansive longing, like a river fed by many smaller streams. This need for openness, this feeling of "aching to be expansive" is found in many of Mish's poems and in many great Oklahoma poems.

Another example is Dean Rader's "Reading Charles Wright in the Year of the Dragon: 33" from his book *Works & Days*. Rader's brand of expansiveness is influenced by experimental, postmodern poets and has as much to do with the avant-garde rejection of closure as it does with Oklahoma's wide-open spaces. Still, the sense of longing toward the infinite seems amplified by the poet's experiences on the Southern Plains, as is suggested in the book's cover photo of a vast field stretching to open sky. The poem ends by contemplating the most expansive being of all:

Eternity is simply the beginning,
everything else is desire.
I want the opposite of desire,
I want to inhabit the other self,
I want to recline in the word *motion*,
I want the secret locked under God's fat tongue.

Poems like this, so open to the writings of others and gesturing in so many ways at once, make of open space, of expansiveness, a yearning. They make of the reader a pioneer looking westward from a rise in the land.

The Oklahoma soul is deep—reticent and expansive. We have struggled, and in our struggles we have learned the art of silence and the value of openness. The qualities that make Oklahoma a great place to live have also given us a great literature.

There is a moment on my daily drive home, a spot near the Pottawatomie/Lincoln county line, when I round a curve and top a hill, suddenly able to see miles ahead and around me. Often I see swaths of charred trees and blackened ground, the scars of grass fires. But I also see pastures dotted with big, round bales of hay. I see livestock and rows of rusted cars and trucks. I see trailer houses and McMansions sprouting from the fields along the highway. I know that just ahead there is a cemetery on my right and, further down the road, a school. I can see miles of field topped with unending sky. I see much, take in much, and I'm speechless. Nearly speechless.

Part IV

B.H. Fairchild

B.H. FAIRCHILD'S ROOTS are in three states of what was once known as the "Great American Desert." He was born in Houston in 1942 and grew up in small towns in Texas, Oklahoma, and Kansas. Fairchild stayed in the region for his education, with degrees from the University of Kansas and the University of Tulsa. His experiences on the plains—work in his father's lathe shop, high school football, hardscrabble living—are at the core of his, mostly narrative, poetry. His poems are full of the oil-field workers and wheat farmers that make up so much of the region's population. But Fairchild's relationship to the plains is deeper than just subject matter. The landscape of the Southern Plains—its unique combination of expansiveness and sparseness—becomes in Fairchild's work a particular kind of poetics, both maximalist and chiseled, emotionally rich but also reticent.

Among prominent contemporary poets, Fairchild stands out for his commitment to narrative verse. Although what the critic Stephen Burt has called "elliptical" poetry—characterized by indirectness, an emphasis on suggestion rather than clarity—dominates much current poetry, Fairchild continues to write in the tradition of Robert Frost, offering the pleasures of good storytelling without compromising the pleasure of poetic craft. The long, roughly hexameter lines that dominate in Fairchild's poetics are flexible and conversational enough to carry a story along, a technique adopted most likely from Frost's reinvention of blank verse as a casual, even folksy medium.

One example of Fairchild's great talent for narrative verse is the poem "Body and Soul," perhaps his best-known poem from what is probably his best book, *The Art of the Lathe*. The poem tells a simple story of an amateur baseball game in Oklahoma in the 1940s, as remembered by a group of old men a generation older than the poet. One player short, the opposing team suggests that they can continue the game if no one objects to a fifteen-year-old kid joining in. The kid turns out to be Mickey Mantle, and not surprisingly, the home team loses. Again, this is a simple story, but Fairchild's genius emerges through the detail accompanying the narrative and through the deeply human significance he is able to draw from it. The poem begins with an image of the men drinking "bourbon and Coke from coffee mugs," a detail almost startling in the accuracy of its observation. The lives of the men are apparent in their "little white rent houses," in their "broken Kenmores," and in "the free calendar from the local mortuary / that said one day was pretty much like another, the work gloves / looped over the doorknob like dead squirrels." The details suggest lives marred by drabness and dreariness, but there is also a dignity to these men who choose to continue pitching to Mantle rather than simply walking him to save the game. They choose, as Fairchild says, to save "some ragged remnant of themselves / to take back home." "But there is one thing more," he adds. The men have been forever changed by encountering "the vast gap between talent and genius." This insight from the poet elevates the narrative from the level of amusing anecdote to the level of universal significance. It becomes a story about men meeting their own limitations, coming to know their own relative smallness, and living on with that difficult truth. This is a very human story.

Fairchild, who is also a scholar of William Blake, frequently writes poems that explore the ways in which the transcendent—the spiritual, the numinous—breaks through into the mundane. He is a visionary poet, and while this visionary aspect in his work has roots in the mystical strand of the Western tradition, it is encouraged by the landscape of the Southern Plains—by the vastness of the ground and the prominence of the sky—a landscape that puts one in constant contact with the eternal. In "Angels," from his first book, *The Arrival of the Future*, a kid home from college "hauling a load of Herefords / from Hogtown to Guymon" sees "four flaming angels crouched on the hood, wings / spread so wide he couldn't see," before he crashes and ends up in the hospital. In the later poem, "Airlifting Horses," ordinary horses become the archetypal Pegasus as they are rescued by helicopter from a brushfire, and "the earth they rode a thousand days or more / falls away in hunks of brown and yellow." Fairchild's poems are often about reclaiming a true vision of the world's holiness, the hidden, dimmed but ever-present wonder of creation.

The best example of Fairchild's unique vision is "Beauty," also from *The Art of the Lathe*. The poem is a good example of Fairchild's fascination with American masculinity and its relationship to the numinous:

> We are at the Bargello in Florence, and she says,
> *what are you thinking?* And I say, *beauty*, thinking
> of how very far we are now from the machine shop
> and the dry fields of Kansas, the treeless horizons
> of slate skies and the muted passions of roughnecks
> and scrabble farmers drunk and romantic enough
> to weep more or less silently at the darkened end
> of the bar out of, what else, loneliness, meaning
> the ache of thwarted desire, of, in a word, *beauty*,
> or rather its absence, and it occurs to me again
> that no male member of my family has ever used

this word in my hearing or anyone else's except
in reference, perhaps, to a new pickup or dead deer.

From this beginning, Fairchild goes on to weave a fugue involving
"rural TV in 1963," a tap-dancing uncle from California, work in a machine shop, J.F.K.'s assassination, exhibitionists, and Donatello's *David*.
It is one of Fairchild's longest poems, and his most clear insistence on
the disruptive value of beauty, its ability to break into the mundane
world and reveal itself as always already present. As in the work of
many mystics, beauty for Fairchild seems always only inches away
from suffering.

Fairchild sees beauty, even holiness, in the sorts of people others
might be tempted to brand as "losers." In this emphasis on the beatific
quality of the seemingly defeated, he is a Dostoevsky of the Southern
Plains. One of the best poems from his first book is "The Woman
at the Laundromat Crying 'Mercy'." The poem ends simply with
"In back, / the change machine has jammed and a woman / beats it
with her fist, crying *mercy, mercy*." There is more than a hint of both
the beatific in general and the Beatitudes in particular in this image.
The later poem, "Old Men Playing Basketball," ends "Boys rise up in
old men, wings begin to sprout / at their backs. The ball turns in the
darkening air." Fairchild looks at desperate women in laundromats
and men long past their physical prime and offers a vision that is
a form of redemption, a way of seeing the world the way it could
be and, according to Christian eschatology, will be. In "Rave On," a
bored teenager driven to entertain himself by deliberately wrecking
cars resurfaces years later in a monastery, a life strangely redeemed by
something even more reckless than the pastimes of bored teenagers.
In the much later "Getting Fired," a man, addressed in the poem in
the second person, returns home after losing his job:

Your friend has her hand on the small
of your back, and you are feeling better now.
The voice of a woman who knew more pain
than any ten professors sings of love gone
wrong and the grace that follows loss.
The changes in a twelve-bar blues are open
doors to her, every chord a new way out.
On a diminished seventh *love*, she says, *love*,
and you pull the blinds, and begin to dance again.

This is a form of grace without a hint of cheapness in it. Maybe this
view of things is "mystical." Maybe it's just a way of seeing that has
kept generations of people sane through hard life on the plains.

The prominence of oil-field workers, horses, and plains in Fairchild's
poems may tempt us to call him a "western writer," but, with his
poems also full of classical music, Renaissance art, and high philosophy, he is as well a Western writer in the sense of having inherited
the high cultural traditions of the Western world. In this he is like
several other prominent poets of the Southern Plains, particularly
Carter Revard and Jim Barnes. It is important to note, however, that
Fairchild's poems travel to Europe the way most of us do, temporarily
or only in the books we read. In "A Roman Grave," the poet observes
"the long cars of the Romanovs" that "move quietly as clouds to line
the curb / of the Russian Orthodox Church in Exile" and reflects
on "[a] Europe of confusions, history's scattered / flocks mumbling
unintelligible prayers." Further on in the poem "he watches diggers
on the Thames' / south side haul up rocks from a Roman grave" and
thinks about the layers of history represented by the "[s]trata piled
like quilts beside the small pits" before concluding that "[t]he dead
in their stone sleep are roused into // history." The poet remains the

outside observer, the American marveling at the layers of the past in Europe, the man in the museum, as in "Beauty." Fairchild perhaps comes closer to the European tradition with his reoccurring character, Roy Eldridge Garcia, who travels to France and becomes a sort of French bohemian poet. Fairchild even writes several poems in the voice of Garcia, prose poems clearly indebted to Baudelaire and Rimbaud. But Garcia comes home: the last of Garcia's prose poems is dated "Liberal, Kansas, 1960." In Fairchild's Southwest, boys hauling cattle carry copies of Rilke. This mixture of high and lower is perhaps most pronounced in his 2009 book, *Usher*, which draws heavily on the work of the Austrian philosopher Ludwig Wittgenstein. The effect of all this mixing of "high" and "low" culture, however, isn't a cloying, second-rate *Wasteland*. One gets the impression, rather, that behind the poems is a real mind, the mind of a boy from the Southern Plains who found, at times, little to do with himself other than to visit the library.

I am tempted to say that Fairchild is *the* great poet of the Southern Plains. But perhaps that would be hyperbolic. There are, of course, others, and there will no doubt be more. Fairchild, however, should be considered the unofficial, yet permanent, poet laureate of the Southern Plains. No other poet I can think of so perfectly captures what life is like here and does it with such artistic integrity and clarity of vision.

Joy Harjo

IN HER LYRICAL and moving memoir, *Crazy Brave*, Joy Harjo remembers standing outside on a starry night with the young Jesuit who was her high school literature teacher at the Institute of American Indian Arts. She says, "He was the first person to talk about the soul to me. He asked me to pay attention to the poetry of living." Readers of American poetry owe much to this anonymous Jesuit, as Joy Harjo has spent her career talking beautifully about the soul to all of us.

And we are, as one of my old teachers might say, in need of a good talking to. English departments in American universities have for far too long avoided the subject of the soul, and the result is a kind of literary education that is fundamentally disoriented and lacking in purpose. Mired in critical philosophies dependent on materialist frameworks, professors of literature have struggled to justify their profession. If the purpose of literary study is merely to foster "critical thinking," would not the subject matter of our philosophy or political science departments better serve that purpose than the poetry of Yeats or Frost? Worse, if the purpose of the literature department were only to debunk, attack, and diminish the achievements of great writers—what we call, following Ricoeur, "the hermeneutics of suspicion"—would it not be better to simply close the doors forever? Although the typical professor of literature would blush to say so, poetry—and novels and plays and films—must speak to the soul if they speak at all, if they are really worth hearing.

This problem of pointlessness has trickled down to affect the study of literature at the high school and even junior high levels, where the only justification we seem able to offer for the reading of books is that it might make students better at math and science. So of course, the audience for poetry continues to dwindle. Why would any adult, with all the math and science classes far behind her, ever again pick up a book of poetry? To adapt Flannery O'Connor's famous quip on the Protestant view of the Eucharist, if that is all it is, then "to hell with it."

But poets like Joy Harjo insist that there is more to it than that, by insisting that there "are more things in Heaven and earth" than historical materialists or deconstructionists dream of in their philosophies. In one of the most moving poems in the book *Conflict Resolution for Holy Beings*, "The First Day Without a Mother," Harjo seems to speak directly to her mother, saying "*I will see you again*," but follows it up, without even breaking the line, with "is one of the names for blue— / a color beyond the human sky of mind." Like the best mystic poets in all traditions, Harjo treats the ineffable as both fact and mystery. The spirit world is as there and as inexplicable as the color blue. (Try explaining "blue" to a colorblind person sometime). Harjo's poems do not offer themselves for easy paraphrase. They have elements of narrative—or at least of narrative situation—but they reveal the story only in glimpses and thus resist simple summation. One might say they are postmodern in this resistance, but Harjo's deep connection to tradition might suggest to us that they are, rather, premodern or post-secular. Harjo does not simply mine the past for pastiche. She carries its weight as a responsibility. "I am carrying over a thousand names for blue that I didn't have at dusk. / How will I feed and care for all of them?" she asks at the end of the poem, indicating the burden that comes with vision. Elsewhere in the same book, in one of the untitled prose poems interspersed throughout, she writes, "I am singing a song that can only be born after losing a country." This loss is a serious matter, and too few contemporary poets can muster the gravitas to address such sorrow. Because Harjo takes the soul seriously, she writes with great authority on suffering.

In Harjo's work, we know the soul is there by the longing it feels. While she does not seem to be a Christian, we can certainly see how her concept of longing and restlessness is reminiscent of Augustine's *Confessions*, where we read that our hearts are restless until they rest in God. The poems in *Conflict Resolution for Holy Beings* repeatedly circle around the concept of longing for home, longing for rest, often conceptualized as "getting back" to an almost prelapsarian past. This theme is familiar to Harjo's longtime readers from previous greatest hits like "Song for the Deer and Myself to Return On" and "Remember." (New readers should see her *How We Became Human: New and Selected Poems: 1975-2001* for an excellent introduction to and overview of her work.) In her newer poems, the urge is often expressed very directly, interrupting the lyrical flow with plain statement. "I will find my way home to you" ends the delicate and lovely "Cricket Song." "Goin' home goin' home" forms the blues-like refrain of another poem. Another musical poem, "One Day There Will Be Horses," ends with a strong sense of yearning: "One day, I will have love enough / To go home." When these poems of longing for home are read alongside *Crazy Brave*, in which Harjo recounts a childhood disrupted by an absent father and a series of lost homes, it is not hard to imagine where this longing originates. Yet Harjo's poetic gift is to turn the personal roots of this sorrowful need into something more universal, something more Augustinian. She does this largely by avoiding direct confessional narrative and instead channeling the poem's emotional energy into image and lyricism. "Every poem is an effort at ceremony," she says in "In Mystic," which begins with the arresting image of "a cross of burning trees, / Lit by crows carrying fire in their beaks." In "For Calling the Spirit Back from Wandering the Earth in Its Human Feet," she says, "Welcome your spirit back from its wandering. It may return / in pieces, in tatters. Gather them together. They will be happy to be found after being lost for so long." For Harjo, the ceremony of return is a ceremony of wholeness.

She also transcends the merely personal by making constant reference to myth, particularly to myths of origin and fall. Harjo titles the first section of *Conflict Resolution for Holy Beings* "How It Came to Be," and it contains multiple origin myths, including "Rabbit Is Up to Tricks," which begins, "In a world long before this one, there was enough for everyone, / Until somebody got out of line." She returns to the prelapsarian theme in "Once the World Was Perfect," and even more inventively in "We Were There When Jazz Was Invented." This interest in returning to the beginning extends throughout the book. The title poem, for instance, ends by imagining a homecoming that blends the New Jerusalem with the restoration of native lands: "When we made it back home, back over those curved roads / that wind through the city of peace, we stopped at the / doorway of dusk as it opened to our homelands." It is, therefore, extremely satisfying when the final poem in the book, "Sunrise," offers a vignette of something like resurrection. "Our bodies were tossed in the pile of kill. We rotted there," the poem's speaker says after detailing a descent into hopeless struggle. But the poem turns unexpectedly toward hope:

> And this morning we are able to stand with all the rest
> And welcome you here.
> We move with the lightness of being, and we will go
> Where there's a place for us.

This restless book comes to rest in a sense of belonging. It is rare to read contemporary poetry with such a sense of hope. Indeed, in most contemporary poetry, even when hope is present, even in Christian poetry, it often seems unearned. Harjo's poems face the darkness, a weight of history and loss, but they also look for transcendence, not by forgetting the things of this world, but by imaginatively redeeming them.

Despite the rare exception of a dud line here and there—one line, "I don't know where I'm going; I only know where I've been," sounds a bit too much like the '80s hairband Whitesnake—*Conflict Resolution for Holy Beings* is an extremely well-crafted book of poems. The imagery is often fresh and astounding, the language full of song. There are personal poems—such as an elegy for the Native American comedian Charlie Hill, and several poems addressing Harjo's children and grandchildren—as well as poems dealing in myth and history. Often, in true visionary fashion, Harjo refuses to separate the personal, the mythic, and the historical. While most of the poems in *Conflict Resolution for Holy Beings* are relatively brief lyrics, they are big-hearted and large-souled. With the prestigious Wallace Stevens Award from the Academy of American Poets and a term as US Poet Laureate under her belt, it is clear that Joy Harjo is a poet of great national significance with true staying power. Perhaps we can take this well-deserved recognition as a sign that soul is making a comeback in literary circles.

Geoffrey Hill

IT IS CURIOUS that Kenneth Haynes, the editor of this new volume of Hill's collected poems, did not see fit to provide an introductory essay. One hesitates, after all, to commence a 973-page journey without even a cursory glance at a map. Also curious is the absence of explanatory notes in a book one assumes aims at being the definitive edition of one of contemporary poetry's most "difficult" poets. With so little scholarly apparatus attached, one wonders what the purpose of a collected works might be. The most obvious answer, and one reason serious readers of contemporary poetry should be grateful to Haynes and to Oxford University Press, is convenience. Hill's work can be difficult to track down in the States, especially if one wants to read all of his previous seventeen books of poems, not counting previous selected poems. This single, readily available, and relatively affordable volume is thus a great kindness to anyone curious as to why Hill is so often referred to as England's greatest living poet.

  Broken Hierarchies also justifies itself by offering four previously unpublished sequences in *The Daybooks*, the multi-volume project comprised of all of Hill's work since 2010's *Oraclau / Oracles*. It is perhaps odd for a collected works to offer so much previously unpublished material, but Hill's readers will nonetheless be grateful for what appears to be the finished arrangement of *The Daybooks*. Also unusual is the amount of revision the author has done on older volumes. As one might expect from an iconoclast like Hill, *Broken Hierarchies* partly justifies its existence as a collected works by troubling our very notion of that category of book.

Perhaps, however, the most important advantage of a collected works is the opportunity it offers for reflecting on the whole of a body of work. By the time Hill's first book, *For the Unfallen*, was published in 1959, the Eliotesque orthodoxy of the impersonal was already giving way to the new "confessional" poetry. It was, after all, the year also of Lowell's *Life Studies*. Yet Hill's earliest work seems, like Lowell's earlier *Lord Weary's Castle*, deeply committed to being "difficult."

Yet Hill's difficulty is not all of one piece. From the high modernism of *The Unfallen* and his second book, *King Log*, Hill turns in the first poem of his masterpiece, *Mercian Hymns*, at least slightly away from new critical ambiguity and toward a more incantatory approach to poetry:

> King of the perennial holly-groves, the riven sandstone: overlord of the
>   M5: architect of the historic rampart and ditch, the citadel at
>   Tamworth, the summer hermitage in Holy Cross: guardian of the
>   Welsh Bridge and the Iron Bridge: contractor to the desirable new
>   estates: saltmaster: moneychanger: commissioner for oaths: marty-
>   rologist: the friend of Charlemagne.
> 'I liked that,' said Offa, 'sing it again.'

The clue to how to read the poem, and the collection, is perhaps given in the last line, a sort of invitation to enjoy the words for the singing of them, the play of sound and image, and not to bother overly much with interpretation. It would not be accurate to say that the poems in this book are any more easily deciphered than those in Hill's first two volumes, although much can be clarified by a reader willing to look up some basics on the reign of Offa, for even with the facts established, there is a certain mystery as to the meaning and purpose of the short poems that make up *Mercian Hymns*, which is to say it is a different kind of ambiguity one finds in this book than in Hill's first two. The effect of the poems is not dependent on the reader's ability to decipher it, to track down the allusions and puzzle out the grammar. These poems are thus arguably more postmodern than modernist, sometimes evoking comparison with John Berryman's *Dream Songs*. Here, for instance, is the first verse paragraph of Hill's eighth hymn:

> The mad are predators. Too often lately they harbor against us. A novel heresy exculpates all maimed souls. Abjure it! I am the King of Mercia, and I know. (90)

And here is the last stanza of Berryman's twenty-second dream song:

> It is the Fourth of July.
> Collect: while the dying man,
> forgone by you creator, who forgives,
> is grasping 'Thomas Jefferson still lives'
> in vain, in vain, in vain.
> I am Henry Pussy-cat! My whiskers fly. (*77 Dream Songs*, 1964)

These poems may stake a little bit of their effect on certain historical information, but much more is staked on inexplicable juxtaposition and shifts in tone: not a puzzle but a mystery. The decision, presumably made by Haynes, to publish *Mercian Hymns* without the notes that accompanied the original edition therefore does little, I think, to change the reader's experience of the poem.

Hill's work also took a personal turn with *Mercian Hymns*. The poems draw richness of detail and authenticity from Hill's childhood in the west midlands, as in the opening of the seventh hymn:

> Gasholders, russet among fields. Milldams, marlpools that lay unstirring.
>   Eel-swarms. Coagulations of frogs; once, with branches and half-bricks,
>   he batter a ditchful; then sidled away from the stillness and silence. (89)

This is the poetics of experience, personal and dynamic however much the specter of Eliot remains. *Mercian Hymns* have much in common with the American experiments of Ashbery, O'Hara, and even Kerouac in turning from a poetics of product to a poetics of process.

And like the best of the postmodernists emerging at midcentury, Hill, in *Mercian Hymns* and to a lesser extent, in 1998's *The Triumph of Love*, crafts an alluring lyricism. This lyricism, alas, is distinctly lacking in Hill's recent work. It is not surprising that *The Triumph of Love* is the best of Hill's later books, as with its emphasis on the overlapping nature of past and present, it is most similar in theme and tone to his earlier masterpiece. Hill's lasting work—drawing both on his childhood in England and on the childhood of England itself—is poignantly caught somewhere between an enriching sense of history and the return of the repressed. Most of our great poets have only one real subject matter. Looking at Hill's collected works it seems apparent to me that he is at his strongest when his focus is most local and specific. Here is the sixth section of *The Triumph of Love:*

> Between bay window and hedge the impenetrable holly
> strikes up again taut wintry vibrations.
> The hellbore is there still,
> half-buried; the crocuses are surviving.
> From the front room I might be able to see
> the coal fire's image planted in a circle

of cut-back rose bushes. Nothing is changed
by the strength of this reflection. (239)

One might almost describe the charm in these lines as "homey,"
though they are not without chill. Then after such vivid, affecting
imagery, one hears in the last two lines an echo of Auden's "poetry
makes nothing happen," with all the complexities and taut ironies
of Auden's phrase.

Backing up a bit, Hill's fourth collection, *Tenebrae,* is full of admirable sentiment and much graceful poetry, but it also marks change, a
movement away from the vivid imagery of *Mercian Hymns,* a decline
even *The Triumph of Love* does not totally recover from. There are still
moments of strong, physical clarity, as in section 6 of the volume's
opening poem, "The Pentecost Castle":

> Slowly my heron flies
> pierced by the blade
> mounting in slow pain
> strikes the air with its cries
>
> goes seeking the high rocks
> where no man can climb
> where the wild balsam stirs
> by the little stream. (117)

On the whole, however, *Tenebrae* is dominated by such abstractions as
that with which Hill closes the section: "there love grows and there
love / rests and is saved" (117). At times, the abstraction sinks to the
level of cliché, as in the eighth section of the same poem:

> And you my spent heart's treasure
> my yet unspent desire
> measurer past all measure
> cold paradox of fire. (117)

There is perhaps a gesture toward imagery here but no concrete reality to solidify the idea. Even in the volume's best-known poem, "'Christmas Trees,'" one feels the vivid and moving opening picture of "Bonhoeffer in his skylit cell / bleached by the flares' candescent fall, / pacing out his own citadel," (137) is nearly spoiled by the pure abstraction of the poem's remaining six lines.

Roughly the last third of *Broken Hierarchies* is occupied by *The Daybooks*, a multi-volume project made up of several previously published books and some books appearing here for the first time. It begins with a preface, titled *Ludo*, and is composed of the following books: *Expostulations on the Volcano, Liber Illustrium Virorum, Oraclau / Oracles, Clavics, Odi Barbare,* and *Al Tempo De' Tremuoti.* It has become a critical orthodoxy that Hill's late work fails to match his earlier work, a dropping off sometimes attributed to the astonishing speed at which the late work has been written in comparison to the relatively slow pace at which Hill produced his earlier masterpieces. This opinion is so widespread as to merit either mockery or confession—it is hard to tell which—from Hill in the fourth section of *Odi Barbare*: "Never again so rightly, / Not again those *marvelous early poems* / Lately acknowledged" (838). There is truth to the charge. A frequent fault in the late work is a tendency to substitute mere vagueness for depth or mystery, as early in *Ludo* where we read:

> A maestro of the hands is not rare;
> nor iron manias.
> Rarer some ironies
> and some brands of despair. (605)

Would it not still be considered a writerly virtue to specify which brands of despair with which we are dealing? Alternatively, the poet might, through an objective correlative, leave the matter sufficiently universal for the reader to supply his or her own version of despair. But the split-difference of the inexact gesture is merely off-putting.

Ludo is at least more readable and inviting than the volumes in *The Daybooks* itself, at times sounding more like Michael Robbins than T. S. Eliot, as when Hill quips in section 46, "You also are feckless. / you should all fuck less / and pray more" (618). *Odi Barbare*, on the other hand, is a thicket of obscure allusions, its syntax so compressed and crabby as to seem intentionally inhospitable. In the final section of the book he seems to refer to his work as requiring from the reader a certain amount of "intelligent patience" (886), but how much time and study does he think he is owed by a reader who could find as much reward at less strain, and with more help from secondary scholarship, by turning back to Virgil, Milton, or Eliot? *Odi Barbare* seems to be hinting toward something about the desire for eternity or stasis or total being, taking Plato as a central figure for this desire. Making a fairly commonplace intellectual issue nearly unintelligible, however, does not add nuance or depth to the commonplace. Perhaps it is fair to say then that the poems demonstrate how bad the influence of Plato's other-worldliness can be for a poet unable to absorb the thought into poetic image, reducing the poems to ever more abstract thought.

Hill has claimed that the difficulty of his work is rooted in his high esteem for the average reader: he expects his allusions to be understood by most people. I am skeptical of Hill's claim to a democratic spirit in his work. He is, at times, rather like the bore one meets at a party, a man who insistently keeps the conversation within his own area of expertise in order to appear well read and informed on all topics. Insisting that the obscure things one happens to know are "common knowledge" is often the tactic of the intellectual bully. Were Hill's references to the wives of Henry VIII or even to prominent figures in the English Civil War, then I might be more inclined to credit his position that "genuinely difficult art is truly democratic." Indeed, Hill's reference to Dante's Paolo and Francesca in section 41 of *Odi Barbare* is fair enough, on the order of Eliot's references to a common cultural legacy. When, however, one discovers that even beginning to understand section 31 of the same poem requires more than a passing familiarity with the work of Belgian avant-garde dramatist Michel de Ghelderode and the inspiration he drew from the Belgian painter James Ensorone, one can't help but be skeptical of Geoffrey Hill as working-class everyman. Surely there is a reasonable parameter to be set for what a poet can expect his reader to bring to the poem, or for, even in the age of Google, what a poet can expect his reader to look up before crossing the line into boorishness. When, in section 14 of the poem, Hill refers to an "Esperanto tract on the Lisbon earthquake" (848), I'm not entirely sure it isn't meant as a description of his work. For this reason, I maintain that, for the most part, open ambiguity—an invitation into mystery, not mere obfuscation—such as that found in *Mercian Hymns*, characterizes Hill's best work and that for which he will certainly be remembered.

But all of *Broken Hierarchies* is worth the considerable amount of time it takes to read it because it covers the career of a poet who continues to matter greatly in contemporary poetics and also because Hill's work continues to take theological matters seriously. From the start, Hill's preoccupation has been with a tenuous, shifting triangulation of violence, history, and God, as seen in his famous early poem "Ovid in the Third Reich" as well as in late work such as section 34 of *Broken Hierarchies'* revised version of *Clavics:*

> Give me your death
> So that I may
> Die briefed; drama
> Hep the nation;
> Contrive well! Fix supply.
> Take it away,
> Your Grace, that folly be made a weird dream
> Of salutation if not salvation,
> Constatation
> Of the cross I woke myself falling from.

Whatever else these lines may convey, they evidence Hill's unflagging concern with theology and violence. Few poets as prominent as Hill take the propositions of Christianity as seriously. Hill's faith, however, is as "difficult" as his verse. In the fifteenth section of *Ludo*, he asks, "How shall I sing the Lord in this strange land? — / if that is my brief / which I doubt." This is an honest and winsome moment in the otherwise often deadening *Daybooks*. That Hill, at eighty-three with twenty-one books of poetry, three volumes of criticism (plus a collected essays), and an appointment as Oxford Professor of Poetry, should pause to question his "brief" is a gesture humble enough to compensate for much of the pedantic boorishness found in his recent poems.

Charles Bernstein

THE PROBLEM with being an experimental poet is that one has to stay experimental in order to stay a poet. When the experiment relies on a particular theory for its fuel, the problem is amplified, for what is there to do after the theory has produced its poem? If one repeatedly mines the same theory for the same sort of poem, one becomes no longer experimental and thus no longer a poet. This is the constant danger faced by the L=A=N=G=U=A=G=E poets, those Wittgensteinian, Derrida-soaked revolutionaries/tricksters of contemporary poetics. *All the Whiskey in Heaven*, a volume of selected poems by the L=A=N=G=U=A=G=E Übermensch, Charles Bernstein, offers, in its thirty-five-year retrospective, a fascinating study in this problem, if not a clear solution to it.

Beginning in the late seventies, a loose group of associates such as Ron Silliman, Lyn Hejinian, and Bernstein set out to create a poetry that radically rejects traditional ideas about speaker and narrative. Their motives were expressly political: by emphasizing language rather than meaning, they hoped to free the reader to construct meaning for herself or himself, thus striking a blow against all forms of hegemony by refusing to impose so much as a pretense of meaning on the reader. Taking their name from the magazine *L=A=N=G-U=A=G=E*, they considered themselves to be the heirs of the American avant-garde, from Louis Zukofsky to John Ashbery.

Bernstein's early poems illustrate all the touchstone characteristics of the L=A=N=G=U=A=G=E experiment: the resistance to narrative, the assault on logic, the abandonment of meaning and closure, the jumpy typography. If the poems in this first part of the selection are unsurprising it is, to be fair, probably their own success, their influence on other poets, that has given them an air of banality. This, too, is the fate of the avant-garde. Perhaps, then, *All the Whiskey in Heaven*, at least for its first one hundred pages or so, is most useful as a primer in L=A=N=G=U=A=G=E poetics. Bernstein would seem to acknowledge as much in his decision to include at the end of the book notes on various poems, mostly revelations of the compositional techniques behind each piece, an addition that gives the volume an air of the school-text. Learning, for instance, that "Asylum" is a collage assembled from a book with the Foucaultian-sounding subtitle *Essays on the Social Situation of Mental Patients and Other Inmates* or that "Lift Off" is transcribed from the correction tape of an IBM type-writer provides the curious reader with clear insight into Bernstein's attempted refutation of the conventionally poetic. These poems answer the classroom question, what does a L=A=N=G=U=A=G=E poet do?

After encountering lines of "poetry" like "HH/ ie,s obVrsxr ; atjrn dugh seineopcv I iibalfmgmMw" from the poem "Lift Off," many readers will conclude that what a L=A=N=G=U=A=G=E poet does is thoroughly confuse and alienate the reader and will thus close the gorgeous cover provided by Farrar, Strauss and Giroux never to open it again. This is a pity because much of what this book has to offer is found later in the volume, in the poems first published in the last decade of the previous century and the first decade of this one. It is in these poems that Bernstein fully embraces the playfulness that is perhaps inherent in the postmodern foundations of his experiment from the start. In other words, he attacks the avant-garde's dilemma by getting in touch with his inner Billy Collins. Unfortunately, the result is sometimes pure shtick, as in the predictable "This Poem Intentionally Left Blank" (which I have just quoted in full).

Not always more successfully, but at least more interestingly, the result is sometimes an experimental poetry that seeks to stay fresh not by seeking new theories or techniques but rather by seeking a variety of means to engage the reader. One technique used several times is to make the poem the occasion and location of its own reflection:

Voice seems

to break

over these

short lines

cracking or

setting loose.

("The Years as Swatches")

While arguably greatly reducing the scope of the poem—something the L=A=N=G=U=A=G=E poets seem to set out to do anyway—such a gesture is reassuring, a gentle promise to the reader that this isn't Pound's *Cantos*, that all one needs to grasp the experiment's handle is there on the page.

The technique is even more pronounced in "This Line":

This line is stripped of emotion.

This line is no more than an

illustration of a European

theory. This line is bereft

of a subject. This line

has no reference apart

from its context in

this line. This line

is only about itself.

Bernstein's clever enjambment, combined with the full view of his naked ars poetica, gives the poem a comic atmosphere that comfortably balances out the post-structuralist pretensions of its thought. Bernstein further invites the reader to relax as he, near the poem's end, openly mocks his own theoretical aspirations:

This line is elitist, requiring,

to understand it, years of study

in stultifying libraries, poring

over esoteric treatises on

impossible to pronounce topics.

The joke is a flexible one, offering to the initiated an insider's joke
that is really a pat on the back for their wide and fashionable reading
and to those outside the mysteries of Derrida and Lacan, an ironic
wink that promises no study is really necessary. While one is unlikely
to be haunted by any given line in a poem like this, it is hard not to
like it. If not a great poem, it is at least an affable poem, which is
often enough.

The poem as its own occasion technique appears again in the later
"Thank You For Saying Thank You," this time as an insiders' laugh
at the expense of readers who laud Ted Kooser's "accessibility" and
who listen faithfully to hear Garrison Keillor share poetry with the
masses on his "Writer's Almanac" program. The joke takes off from
the first line:

This is a totally

accessible poem.

There is nothing

in this poem

that is in any

way difficult

to understand.

One thinks of Ashbery's similarly tongue-in-cheek "Paradoxes and Oxymorons," which begins with the claim that "[t]his poem is concerned with language on a very plain level." While Ashbery's oft-anthologized poem, however, goes on to develop the joke into a surprisingly tender reflection on the ontological gap between poet and reader, Bernstein's poem goes on simply to repeat the joke in ninety mercifully short lines. The poem fails because it never moves beyond the cheap gesture of shared condescension. The same may be said for poems like "Foreign Body Sensation," which begins with the comically forthright statement "I am especially interested in the treatment of depression. With my Lord and Savior Jesus Christ at the center of my life, I have found real Joy and Purpose in dedicating myself to the Truth of His Teaching as Written in the Bible." The joke depends upon the shared assumption between poet and reader that we are not those people. These poems have little to offer the reader beyond the schoolyard or faculty club affirmation of a strained superior laughter.

To his credit, Bernstein seems aware that this strategy isn't sustainable long term and gives some indication of movement in a different direction in the book's only new poem, the envoi and title poem, "All the Whiskey in Heaven." What to make of this last poem may be the most pressing question for reviewers of this book. Considering the L=A=N=G=U=A=G=E poets' rejections of the lyric "I," this last poem seems to be surprisingly earnest. The final stanza is almost embarrassingly frank:

No, never, I'll never stop loving you

Not till my heart beats its last

And even then in my words and my songs

I will love you all over again

While the lack of punctuation in these lines might strain toward some sort of experimental facade, the sentiment is shockingly commonplace and the poetry is shockingly bad. Each of these four lines seems to revel in its own triteness. Is it possible that Bernstein, with nowhere left to go in the experimental direction, finds himself forced back into conventional territory only to find he has no actual poetic talent at all? Or is it the most avant-garde statement of all, an abandonment of the last narrative standing, that of the poem's own antagonistic relationship to tradition? Or is Bernstein calling us to question the very notion of good poetry and bad poetry? Of course, these questions only matter if one reads poetry in order to meditate on poetics, if one only cares about this poem for what it says about poetry. Taken at face value, it's just a bad poem.

All the Whiskey in Heaven is an important book because it collects a sample from a body of work that has usefully challenged the complacency of mainstream poetry. Bernstein's work provides interest, provokes thought, and occasionally amuses. If it fails to offer all that one might go to poetry seeking, it faithfully serves its side in a dialectic between the experimental and the "accessible" that gives much vigor to contemporary American poetry and poetics. It serves both as a helpful primer on the history of the contemporary avant-garde and as an open question about the future of L=A=N=G=U=A=G=E poetry. It does not, however, represent the future of poetry in general, one hopes.

Jeanne Murray Walker

Jeanne Murray Walker's *Helping the Morning: New and Selected Poems* is a very welcome overview of the career of a major Christian poet. Walker, along with other poets of her generation, such as Scott Cairns and Paul Mariani—whose selected works were published in 2006 and 2012, respectively—has done much to bring together Christian literary pursuits and the mainstream of American poetry. She is a writer both deeply spiritual and thoroughly contemporary, and her poems have shown many younger Christian writers a path for pursuing their work with both religious and literary integrity. In the first section of *Helping the Morning*, she offers new poems that live up to her reputation for vivid, fresh images in poems that call us to view the world as sacred. At the end of "Miniature Song of Complaint," for instance, she says, "I can almost see us from the road, our tiny house, / hanging like one last gold leaf in the oak tree." This sense of beauty and fragility in precarious balance imparts to her work a wisdom far beyond the mere didacticism which tempts many Christian writers.

One of the pleasures of a selected works, especially one as well edited as this, is watching a poet come into her own as a writer. In Walker's case, this includes a growth in wisdom that is closely aligned with a growth in craft and art. To put it in slightly clichéd terms, the reader watches her find her voice. One sees in Walker's early poems much promise and talent, but it is often overshadowed by obvious influences. Walker seems to begin her career, like many poets of her generation, in the shadow of Sylvia Plath. Take, for instance, these lines from "Praying for Father on All Saints' Day":

> But I am done with you,
> my dodge, my fleet dead. I have come to give
> you up, my strong ghost, my sweet parent
> long since pushed into the ground as into an oven.

Apostrophe to a dead father isn't necessarily a signal of confessional allegiance, but the nature of the address, the atmosphere of an exorcism, is distinctly Plathian. "I am done with you" is nearly quotation from Plath's "Daddy," and the allusion in the image of the oven is unmistakable. Although the father-daughter relationship in this poem doesn't seem as fraught as in *Ariel*, Plath's dramatic and violent imagery seems to dominate the poem, as when she evokes Plath's jackbooted "panzer-man": "Burn / until not a button is left, not the sound / of a boot stamping in autumn air." Coming to this volume with an awareness of Walker's later achievement, one gets great pleasure in watching the younger poet struggle to assimilate the strong voices that influenced so many writers of her generation.

By the time of 1985's *Fugitive Angels,* Walker seems to be following the general movement of mainstream American poetry toward a mild surrealism under the influence of John Ashbery, who had recently added the Bollingen to his Pulitzer and National Book Award. Walker, better than many of Ashbery's many imitators, picks up the emotional possibilities of surrealism, the sad, soft music of Ashbery's best poems, and foregrounds it in poems like "For my Daughter's Twenty-First Birthday":

> I stroked her cheek with my finger,
> and she began to suck for dear life,
> like a fish in the last stages of suffocation above water.
> When I poured my voice down to revive her,
> she grinned and graduated from college
> summa cum laude, schools of minnows parting before her.
> "You are not a fish," I said to her.
> "You are my daughter, and just born, too.

This is not quite the subtle and resonant voice Walker will bring to her finest poems, but it is an effective and moving piece. Surrealism will not, ultimately, be the path Walker takes in her best work, but she will absorb from it a penchant for striking and dramatic images, for seeing the world afresh.

Arguably Walker's own voice, one quieter and perhaps more subtle than either Plath or Ashbery, arrives with 1990's *Coming into History*, in which striking images bring movement and color to the surface of poems that, through the exercise of great restraint, convey a sense of profound depth. A good example of this quality is "The Shawl." The poem begins simply and compellingly:

> Somewhere on Ellis Island
> my mother's mother lost the shawl
> the women of the town crocheted for her
> out of mauves and purples,
> old tunes twisted in the strands,
> and clever plots
> woven, woven in the pattern.

The poem then accelerates through history, creating through the propulsion of the verse—short lines dominated by stressed syllables,

as in "whose leaves clinked down / like foreign coins"—a sense of
inevitable progression as the family moves west and as each generation
gives way to the next. Near the end of the poem she describes the
grandmother figure in these simple but breathtaking lines:

> finally carrying
> her children's
> children on her hip
> while she stirred the soup,
> their breath soft as moss,
> their tiny feet stuttering against her.

Much matter of great importance is captured here with a few
well-chosen words. The visual repetition figured in the "stuttering
feet," for instance, beautifully reinforces the suggestion of repetition
with difference in "children's / children," which is, by the way, a great
example of a meaningful line break in the way it dramatizes continuity and change. This kind of serious craft and deep art is abundant
throughout Walker's four books leading up to this collected edition. I
would particularly point the reader to "Nursing," "Talking to the Baby
about Taking the Bus," "So Far, So Good," and "Making the Move."
    At the center of Walker's best work is an exploration of empa-
thy. This exploration first comes to the foreground of her poetics in
Stranger Than Fiction (1992), a collection of dramatic monologues
giving voice to various characters inhabiting the pages of supermarket tabloids. Walker poetically inhabits the lives of, for instance, an
invisible girl, a man whose thumb bleeds for three years, an heiress
who starves to death, and a beauty queen who gives birth to a monster.
These poems are interesting—by turns amusing and poignant—and
always well executed. Yet even in the hands of a master like Robert
Browning, the dramatic monologue is inherently limited in its ability

to generate empathy. Even when the monologue is most sympathetic to its subject, it is still very conspicuously an act of ventriloquism. The monologue form thus undermines the act of empathy by offering the illusion of leaping over the distance between two people, poet and character, rather than engaging in the hard work of crossing that distance. While the effort is noble, the poetic strategy in *Stranger Than Fiction* ultimately points to the inherent limits of literary empathy. The monologue offers only a cardboard cutout of the empathetic imagination.

In her best, later poems, Walker turns this limitation into a powerful virtue in poems that enact the difficult, but crucial, struggle to wade across—with no shortcuts—the divide between any two people. In "The Failing Student" a teacher says to herself, in response to the student, "You begin picking your way toward her / through a whole vocabulary / of wildflowers and thorns." The poem, in its halting rhythms and thorny images, dramatizes that effort toward connection. In my favorite of her poems, "Gesture Upwards," Walker begins, again simply, with "I have promised to pray for a friend / the way one promises when there are no solutions." The rest of this poem, full of vivid and emotionally effective images, is occupied with the poet attempting to find her way to that prayer, attempting to connect with her friend and with God despite how "Here in Vermont the cold is slowing things down / the way a squad car parked along the shoulder / slows traffic." That is, despite how the world goes on in a beautiful and heartless indifference. At the poem's end, we are given this stunning glimpse: "Like the sole of a foot, a yellow leaf / steps on the windshield, then another, / and another, like feet, walking on water." In this powerful image, the poet seems to find connection with Christ, and thus presumably achieve at least silent prayer for the friend. In the image of the natural world, however, this connection is a mediated, an ambiguous or limited connection. It is an honest connection and sacramental in its orientation.

Speaking of sacrament, reading these poems from Walker's last four collections, along with the new poems included at the beginning of the volume, I am constantly reminded of Allen Tate's neglected but brilliant essay "The Man of Letters in the Modern World," in which he distinguishes between the mere "communication" that abounds in our consumer culture and the real "communion" that is at the heart of true literature. Tate writes, "Perhaps it is not too grandiose a conception to suggest that works of literature, from the short lyric to the long epic, are the recurrent discovery of the human communion *as experience*, in a definite place and at a definite time." Walker, in her carefully crafted and vivid poems, fulfills that challenging call to a renewed, ever contemporary and specific communion as well as any poet writing today.

Mary Oliver

IT IS FASHIONABLE to disdain the "accessibility" of certain popular poets, Mary Oliver chief among them. The problem with *A Thousand Mornings*, however, is not its "accessibility" but rather its smugness and its reliance on cliché.

These poems repeatedly come to rest in self-congratulations. "If I were a Sufi for sure I would be / one of the spinning kind" Oliver proclaims with a pat on her own back at the end of "If I Were." In "Good-Bye Fox" she ventriloquizes nature for the purpose of self-affirmation: "you're okay in my book," says the fox in response to the poet's wit. Oliver is certainly "okay" throughout her own book as well. In "The Moth, the Mountains, the Rivers" she preaches outright: "Strange questions, yet I have spent worthwhile time with them. And I suggest them to you also, that your spirit grow in curiosity, that your life be richer than it is, that you bow to the earth as you feel how it actually is." Leaving aside the artless use of the prose poem form, these lines would be groan-inducing even in a graduation speech. Worse is "Three Things to Remember," which begins with "As long as you're dancing, you can / break the rules" and then immediately concludes with "Sometimes breaking the rules is just / extending the rules. // Sometimes there are no rules." One fears this may be what Facebook and Twitter can do to contemporary poetry: cheap wisdom, cheaply expressed.

"You fuss over life with your clever / words, mulling and chewing on its meaning," that talking fox affectionately chides Oliver, but the charge does not hold up. This metaphor of chewing on meaning is itself among the most worn out of clichés. In "The First Time Percy Came Back" we are told that the dead dog is "unreachable. As music / is present yet you can't touch it." Such easy sentimentality is a betrayal of the poem's emotional stakes (compare the two ho-hum elegies for Oliver's Percy to Mark Doty's devastating pet elegies in *School of the Arts*). A few flashes here and there suggest that Oliver is still capable of arresting images well expressed but, in most cases, has not sufficiently bothered to search for the stronger, fresher line. She has, to borrow from Yeats, failed to "lie down where all the ladders start."

An exception is the remarkable "Hum, Hum," which mines childhood pain in a powerful and well-made poem. "Hum, Hum" succeeds by offering more ambiguity than the typical Oliver poem. Rather than the facile praise of mystery which typifies her work, this poem enacts mystery, from the surprise arrival of bees in the beginning, through a dark past, to a pressing onward at the end. If the stakes were this high in at least a few other poems in *A Thousand Mornings*, it would be a worthwhile book indeed. As is, I recommend the issue of *Five Points* in which "Hum, Hum" first appeared.

Paul Mariani

PAUL MARIANI is a haunted man. Perhaps we are all haunted, but what is impressive about Mariani is his willingness to admit it, his openness about the ghosts in his life. Take for example the preface to his brilliant biography of John Berryman, *Dream Song*, in which he describes a shadowy figure who emerges from the Freudian/Dantean realm he calls "the dark underworld of the imagination" to pursue Mariani and impress upon him the obligation to write the book that would be *Dream Song*. Such frankness about one's ghosts, such willingness to break the academic posture of objectivity, is rare enough to be precious to any reader, and the value of this frankness is in the resulting clear view of the most troubling thing about ghosts: they always have a claim on us. They speak to us of commitments that go deeper than the commitments of our own making. It is perhaps, then, their proximity to us rather than alienation from us that makes ghosts so frightening. In *Epitaphs for the Journey*, Mariani's volume of "New, Selected, and Revised Poems," his ghosts are on display in poems that are both intimate and learned, that time and again circle poetically around the deep claims laid on the poet's soul by the ghosts of time past.

Like Berryman, and like so many of us, Mariani is haunted by the ghost of his father, a spirit he addresses directly in "Crossing Cocytus," a poem that is clearly an attempt to put the old man to rest.

The word *father* appears in no less than six titles of poems selected for the volume, and the very first poem in *Epitaphs for the Journey,* "Mairzy Doats," calls up the ghost of the poet's father, summoning the "Recording Angel" to "rewind" the tape of Mariani's life to a moment when he was a small boy, sitting in the back seat while his father and his father's brother conversed up front in the strange dialect of adults, mixed in the child's mind with the nonsense coming from the radio. He is, however, unable to remain in that back seat for long; "the flecked film / frozen in blacks and whites and sepias, like some / Roman ruin crumbling on a darkling plain" breaks up, and the poet is propelled back into the present, dragging with him two ghosts: "these two who follow me / everywhere I go[.]" The follower, the child in the back seat yearning for adult understanding, has become the followed, pursued by ghosts who make claims upon the present, who demand, in Mariani's own words, "to be fed" their food, the attention of the living. In *Hamlet,* "Remember me" is, after all, the chief demand that the old ghost makes upon the young prince of Denmark.

Mariani is haunted as well by the ghosts of former selves, the shades of lives he lived before. In poems that make moving meditations out of the fragmented memory of early youth, Mariani holds a séance to summon the ghosts of his own childhood self. We might ask, if the claim of dead fathers is to our attention, then what claim do these dead selves of childhood have on us? Perhaps it is the claim to explanation, the demand that we make right the confusion of youth by sifting and sorting things from the vantage point of the present. If so, it is a claim the poet can never quite make good on, for to explain the past, he must imaginatively enter into it, losing the clarity of the present, allowing himself to be possessed by the specter of the earlier self. One fine example is "The Furnace: July

1945," which begins with the confusion of a child who wakes in the
night to a malfunctioning furnace shaking the floor "until the bed
itself begins to tremble" (an image anyone who has seen *The Exorcist*
might be prone to associate with a kind of haunting) and ends in
the deeper, unresolved confusion of a child looking up at a sky full
of bombers on their way to Europe or Japan, a child who turns to
his military father for answers but is left unable to fully comprehend
the meaning of seeing "the heavens darkened with those / avenging
angels he kept telling me were friends." Other poems look at later
stages of adolescence, such as sexual awakening and first jobs, but still
give the sense of an earlier self that haunts the present demanding
an explanation. Many of Mariani's best reflections on childhood
and young adulthood remind us that if, as Wordsworth would have
it, "the child is father to the man," then this ghostly father, too, cries
out "remember me."

   As one progresses further into Mariani's selected works, the nature of the ghosts shifts in ways appropriate with age. Many poems
focus on his children because, though we usually associate ghosts
with the past, to be a father is to be haunted by the future. We see
also many poems in which Mariani is haunted by his literary prede-
cessors—Berryman, William Carlos Williams, Hopkins, Dante—as
one might expect a prominent biographer, critic, and poet to be.
One might, in a less strident version of the "anxiety of influence,"
posit that these poets, along with the several intellectual mentors
evoked elsewhere in the book, are father figures, rehearsing their
own claims on their poet descendant. But the most prominent father in *Epitaphs for the Journey* is God the father, because most of
all Mariani is God-haunted. Mariani's poems are never abstractly
theological; rather they offer glimpses of God between the cracks of
regular human life. His straightforward delivery—generally, though
not always, in plain-style free verse—helps to cement this sense of

the ordinary. But in Mariani's best poems, the sacred, the ineffable, comes slipping in, haunting the world of regular life. No poem better illustrates Mariani's God-haunted sensibility than the powerful and masterfully structured "Quid Pro Quo." The poem begins with an account of the poet's wife in the hospital again after the second of two miscarriages in four months. Asked by a colleague what he thinks of God now, Mariani offers "a variant / on Vanni Fucci's figs" by "raising [his] middle finger up to heaven, *quid / pro quo.*" But God does not, it seems, take the hint, and He continues to haunt Mariani, following the young couple the summer after to a "cedar-scented cabin off Lake George" where they apparently conceive a son, "a little Buddha-bellied / rumplestiltskin runt of a man who burned / to face the sun." As this sweeping poem moves toward its conclusion, we learn that this gift of a child grows up to become a priest, prompting the poet to ask "How does one bargain / with a God like this, who, *quid pro quo,* ups / the ante each time He answers one sign with another?" This ghostly father is as unshakable as he is unpredictable.

In critical works like *God and the Imagination,* in biographies ranging in subject from Williams to Berryman to Hopkins, in six previous volumes of poetry, Mariani's contribution to the Christian literary community and to the broader sphere of American letters has been significant. *Epitaphs for the Journey* provides a much-needed look back over his poems from the last thirty-four years, offering the reader a fine array of heartfelt and haunted lyrics prompting us to think about the demands our ghosts make upon us. Despite an increasingly consumer-oriented culture that would do away with ghosts by reducing all time to the eternal present of the purchase, may we all be as richly, blessedly haunted as Paul Mariani.

Joe Weil

I'M DRIVING north on Oklahoma Highway 18 with Joe Weil in the passenger seat and his wife and infant daughter in the back. Joe is pointing out all the commonalities between central Oklahoma and his neck of the woods, New Jersey: the invasive eastern cedars, the red-tinted dirt, the working poor. He's come 1400 miles to read at my little university just because he's always wanted to see Oklahoma and even though he's certainly losing money on the trip. Our previous acquaintance consists of sharing a publisher—NYQ Books—and a Facebook friendship, the highlight of which was Joe's advice about a cracked engine block in my old car (it turned out not to be a cracked engine block). Nevertheless, here he is, tooling up Highway 18, getting the grand tour of my homeland, talking about how much he has enjoyed meeting the students at our little college, smiling, gesturing excitedly: because he's open and generous like that. He's big-hearted like that. He is completely present, very incarnated like that. And his poems share all these qualities, which is why you should read his new and selected poems, *The Great Grandmother Light*.

Like Joe himself, Weil's poems don't shy away from showing emotion. In "Adelino" he talks about "Wolf songs," songs that "could / pull down a man and feed on his heart," an image that conveys well the emotional power of many of the poems in this book. The poem "Fists," for instance, is a moving account of the poet's complex relationship with his father. Rather than offering merely pure, "raw" emotion, however, the poem draws deeper emotional resonance by evoking the tale of Cuchulain's accidental slaying of his own son:

> When he woke, it was morning, and the hands of his son
> Had become two black swans.
> They flew west where all suffering ends.
> I read this story
> And I remember you.
> Hold me clenched until I am those birds.
> Sleep now,
> Until your fists can open.

Other poems look further beyond the poet's own experiences, illustrating Weil's great capacity for empathy as he imagines his way into the lives of people he meets along the way. "An old man tells me about Cuba. / Drunk, he talks of dice / and mangoes," begins the poem "At the My Fair Lady Lounge." In "Dignity" he offers sympathy for the, perhaps inebriated, elderly woman who has just run over a dog. When I praise the empathetic ability of these poems, I mean to praise it not only as an ethical virtue but also as an aesthetic virtue. This empathy opens the poems to a broad range of compelling imagery: for instance, the berated and "perfectly bald husband / swinging his garden hose violently / in futile protest" in "The Poet as a Young Voyeur." These are big-hearted poems, poems open to the world and to feeling. If a lot of contemporary poems walked into your neighborhood bar and sat down next to you, you'd probably get up and leave. You could smell the narcissism and claustrophobic creepiness. I would, however, like to buy a beer for any number of poems by Joe Weil.

Joe's reputation is as a "working class poet," and you will certainly find many poems in *The Great Grandmother Light* drawing on factory work and life on the economic margins of middle-class America. But the collection also adds nuance and complication to the "working-class poet" label. These poems are often intellectual and always well read. They bear particularly clear influence from the American avant-garde and from the French surrealism that in turn influenced it. For instance, in the early poem "Prelude" he tells us "this is my hand, / writhing into the void, / pulling up rabbits, / the beloved dead." In the much later prose poem "Green Light" we are made to understand that "the voice of the midnight universe is always vaguely Southern" and that "pain calcifies in the heart, how great cathedrals in the cave of someone's closed eyes are being formed—drop by drop, on the limestone walls of trout streams, in the caves of Kentucky." Consistently Weil displays his awareness that poetry is and should be a strange thing. Unlike many other poets aiming for a working-class ethos, he doesn't achieve his accessibility and relevance by sacrificing surprise and playfulness. He doesn't mistake mere mundanity for authenticity. Joe is not some hipster in a work shirt who has read a bit of Whitman and a few poems by Philip Levine, trying to make "working class" a marketable niche. He's a real poet whose context happens to be working class and who knows, like Charles Dickens and Frank O'Hara knew, that his context, his world, is the great subject he has been given and to which he must fashion his own stylistic response. "I, too, grew up in this neighborhood," he says in "Variations on a Theme by Isaiah," after encountering a particularly unpleasant "little bastard" in his old neighborhood. But the ending of the poem illustrates how these poems do more than simply recount "gritty realities," the go-to move for lesser poets looking to distinguish themselves from the middle-class crowd coming out of the MFA workshops. When Weil writes "God bless that angry little shit. / God bless this angry little shit. / This, too, is a poem of praise," he displays an authenticity beyond simple "street cred," a genuine desire to see eternity and redemption in his own specific, concrete world.

Mention of eternity and redemption brings me to the heart of this book, because Joe's poems constantly ache with an awareness of the sacred, though they never look for sacredness in the never-never lands of always elsewheres or not-yet-but-somedays of lesser religious poetry. Joe's sacred is the Catholic sacred of the sacramental, of the holy entering this world and changing it while not changing it. In the early poem "Morning at the Elizabeth Arch" poetic vision itself is a form of redemption:

> The winos rise as beautiful as deer.
> Look how they stagger from their sleep
> as if the morning were a river
> against which they contend.
>
>   . . .
>
> At river's edge, the deer stand poised.
> One breaks the spell of his reflection
> with a hoof and, struggling,
> begins to cross.

The winos are both themselves and deer, as the bread is both bread and the body of Christ. The *look* is our invitation to take and eat. "While the World Is Falling Apart, I Open a Jar of Pickles" is another fine example, a poem in which incense is replaced by "the fragrant scent of pickling / spices wafting over" the poet. Joe invests a simple, humble, and homely act with the spiritual power of sacrament, "opening a jar against all evils, the / stupid deaths, and illnesses, and failures." This sacrament is an act of desperation and trust that makes him, to adapt Jesus' words in Matthew 18:3, like a little child, or to put it in Joe's own terms, "a little boy in the near dark, bare foot / against the scarred linoleum." The "near dark" is clearly more than a dimly lit kitchen and more than the linoleum has been or will be scarred. But, he says, "If you slice these thin enough / the veil becomes translucent." This image literalizes holy light shining *through* the things of this world. Auden has taught us that "the crack in the tea-cup opens / a lane to the land of the dead," but this is the only poem I know of in which spiritual reality is revealed by means of a pickle. It's a strange sacrament—aren't they all?—but it's enough. His heart, which had earlier beat out in defiance—"fuck it all, fuck it all"—now beats in submission to an invisible order, to a knowledge of its own child-like dependence: "My heart is the only justice. It is strong. / It will do its job. It will knock and knock / until the door is opened." This is not cheap grace or glib Jesus talk. It is a few simple words on the virtue of life rafts, penned by a man who has been far out to sea.

Back on Highway 18, Joe is telling me about his childhood, its imaginative joys and emotional suffering. He is telling me about how happy he is to be fulfilling his dream of visiting Oklahoma, wide-open spaces for his wide-open heart and his wide-open poems. Joe Weil is a man who, as Montaigne said of himself, is "consubstantial with" his book, or perhaps transubstantial, like those winos and deer. In the devastatingly tender—yes, I said "devastatingly tender"—"About Light," young Joe, who has just asked his mother "why are the traffic lights more red when it snows," is told, "keep yourself a secret. / People will spit on you." Praise be to God that Joe does not follow that well-meant advice.

C. K. Williams

WHEN C. K. WILLIAMS died, he left behind more than half a century's worth of superb work as well as a sterling reputation attested to by a Pulitzer Prize, a National Book Award, and a National Book Critics Circle Award. Williams has always been a versatile poet—like his hero, Whitman, he contained multitudes—but he was best known early in his career as a political poet in the Vietnam era. His later work still contains much political and cultural commentary—*The Singing*, with selections included in this volume, is his most political of the late works—but as this collection of his *Selected Later Poems* shows, Williams is a poet of meditation, more in the tradition of the inwardly focused Donne and Herbert than of public poets like Dryden or Pope. Especially in his later works, Williams transcends the merely "confessional" to become one of America's greatest poets of the meditative, personal lyric.

Williams' famous long lines, a poetics he shifted to in the 1970s, augment this meditative quality in his best work. While Williams derived this sweeping line from Whitman's expansive verse, the effect is very different from that of his predecessor. In Whitman's poetry, as in that of his close descendants like Allen Ginsberg, the long line creates an effect of breathless prophecy, a poetics for men with beards. Withholding breath until the end of the line, Whitman becomes a Jeremiah proclaiming truth to all, literally breathless with vision. Williams' long lines, however, are more casual: not so much breathlessness as breathing room. The difference is part diction and imagery but also part syllable count. Whitman pushed past the standard pentameter line but not so far as to lose the gravitational pull of the standard ten syllables. The effect was like a rubber band stretched taut. Williams, however, goes a bit further in line length, so that the pull of gravity shifts from the pentameter all the way to prose, stretching the rubber band until its elasticity gives out.

This looseness results not in slackness but in openness, a line that can accommodate a long and shifting string of thoughts and things. In his essay "A Letter to a Workshop," included in his prose collection *In Time*, Williams defends the poet's right to abstraction, and he often in these later poems indulges in long strings of winding thought, as in "Soul in Steel": "Not frail not fainthearted flighty and I certainly don't mean merely to mean unmale with those now / happily unacceptable connotations of frivolous faithless flirty emphatically no innuendo like that / I mean rather shouldn't I be able to conceive a yes unmale soul for this bundle of matter and pain. . . ." The lack of punctuation mirrors the looseness of thought—a stream of consciousness technique—but each line is given integrity by heavy alliteration and frequent syllabic accent.

Yet despite his defense of abstraction, Williams is also a poet of particulars, opening up his long lines to include a multitude of the things of this world. "House," for instance, begins, "The way you'd renovate a ruined house, keeping the 'shell,' as we called it, brick, frame, or stone, / and razing the rest: the inside walls—partitions, we say—then stairs, pipes, wiring, commodes." The list asserts the reality, even as they are removed, of all the trappings of the domestic world in which so many of Williams' poems take place. Often a line in Williams' late poems will offer a catalog that seems in tune not so much with the Homeric, epic catalog of Whitman as with the old Sears Roebuck catalog, offering a bit of everything but nothing over-sensationalized.

Critics often describe Williams' lack of sensationalism as "detachment," and that is a good description as long as one does not take it to mean coldness or indifference. Rather, the dispassionate tone is a way of building emotional urgency in the poem without slipping into sentimentality. As Tony Hoagland said of Jack Gilbert, "It's the angle between the verbal style and the subject matter that energizes the drama and forms the tone here: a sort of passionate stoicism" (*Real Sofistikashun*, 2006). Williams' "passionate stoicism" is a great vehicle for a wide range of meditations: from the crude humor of "Gas," which is about exactly what it sounds like, to the domestic sublime of the late poems for his wife, Catherine. Death and sex are both frequent topics in Williams' work, and both are handled without romanticism or hysteria but with compassion and gravity, a gravity sometimes willed up poetically out of the absurdity of life.

This is a humane poetry, which reveals the reason one feels that, even with such a prolific body of work and such a long and accomplished career, we lost C.K. Williams too soon. This volume is a consolation.

Alfred Corn

ALFRED CORN is a virtuoso, and with his new collection's formal variety and impressive wit, *Tables* would have, in an earlier age, made an excellent appeal for patronage. It's a shame that today's great patrons of the literary arts, the universities, care little for virtuosity and much for credential and prestige, because, with the support of a Maecenas or a Cangrande della Scala or a Lady Elizabeth Carey, Alfred Corn could be the best-known poet of his generation. As is, he hasn't been without acclaim—praise from Harold Bloom for his first book, a Guggenheim in '86—but Corn himself, at several moments in *Tables*, expresses a sense of having been passed over by those who bestow the laurels. In "Letter to Robert Pinsky," Corn contrasts his own career fortunes with those of the former poet laureate, noting that the gods of fame have had only "offhand ways" with him but also expressing admiration for Pinsky's poems and gratitude for the friendship. Corn is perhaps rueful of his own fate but doesn't seem bitter toward the more "successful" poet. "We might have been mere rivals. *Are* long-term / Friends," he says near the end of the poem. In another poem, "Window on the World," the tone is a bit more bitter, though also wry, the poet confessing that "envy sometimes hissed, / Those years I spent cooling my heels outside fame's shortlist," and naming several other poets who, at the time of Corn's debut volume, were "rated the latest star." Sometimes caustic, sometimes resigned,

Corn is as self-conscious of his own "rank" as John Berryman was throughout his turbulent career but possessed of a better sense of perspective than Berryman perhaps ever managed to develop. For instance, Corn's concerns about his career in "Window on the World" dissolve quickly when memories of the attack on the World Trade Center enter the poem. Corn is perhaps typical of our time in his obsession with fame, but he is rescued by a humane perspective and a sympathetic imagination from the self-absorption that usually comes with that obsession.

Corn, of course, has achieved a level of fame as the author of the *The Poem's Heartbeat*, one of the best and best known of the various manuals on prosody and form. It is thus not surprising that Corn's virtuosity in traditional meter and forms is on display throughout this book. He uses blank verse, couplets, modified forms of both the sonnet and the ghazal, elegiac quatrains, an approximation to classical hexameters, prose, and free verse. Such variety on its own may not be impressive, but Corn's ability to sound natural and self-assured in so many different forms is very impressive indeed. He is, for instance, as capable of stately blank verse in "St. Anthony in the Desert"—"To be filled with that hallowed emptiness / The hermit sojourns in a desert cave"—as he is of fluid and graceful heroic couplets in "First Dictionary":

> That bedside ark, no tub or leaky dud,
> offered warm shelter in the mounting flood.
>
> Where Noah housed his couples, aardvark, zebu,
> And—I think unpolluted—my kind, too.

Elsewhere in the book, Corn's free verse is strengthened by his prosodic intelligence. For instance, "Horizontal," the collection's opening poem, works generally through a free verse minimalism evocative of Carl Phillips or perhaps Franz Wright, including extra spacing, but begins with a trochaic pulse to set an incantatory tone. Two lines later the poem slips into a line of perfect iambic pentameter as a sort of foil for the free verse that dominates the poem. Corn ends the poem with one more line of smooth pentameter, giving the poem a sense of closure that strains interestingly against the expectations of open-endedness established by the minimalist approach.

Along with formal virtuosity Corn exhibits an even rarer virtue: awareness of the variety of occasions for a poem. The combined force of Wordsworth's famous dictum about "emotion recollected in tranquility" and the broad appeal of confessional poetics has arguably left contemporary poetry with a flattened sense of occasion. Corn, however, offers us poems that spring from a number of occasions. For instance, he includes the much-neglected verse epistle among the modes in which he demonstrates his virtuosity, composing one each to James Fenton, Grace Schulman, Robert Pinsky, and Marilyn Hacker. He also includes a poem for Joseph Brodsky that, while not explicitly an epistle, evokes the letter form in its cozy apostrophe to the other poet and in its focus on a shared memory with Brodsky. Corn accomplishes in these poems much that one expects from the personal lyric—reminiscences rueful and delightful, arresting imagery drawn from the details of a particular scene, meditations on the ego and its place in historical movement, declarations of love and regret—but the epistolary mode adds a certain sense of fresh and open air, of correspondence rather than mere monologue, despite the fact that we never hear the other voice. Perhaps this effect is achieved by the epistle's assumption that there *is* another voice, another person outside the solipsism of much contemporary poetry.

Accompanying this avoidance of solipsism in *Tables* is a focus

throughout on hospitality. Corn's letter to James Fenton begins
with what appears to be an allusion to Jonson's "Inviting a Friend
to Supper":

> James, transposing the stock opening
> in which letter-despatcher invites
> a friend to dinner, let me begin
> with thanks for lunch at Long Leys Farm—and
> for coming to fetch me at the steps
> of the Ashmolean in Oxford.

Corn's fine sense of occasion is exhibited as well in several other
poems which, in classical style, take the shared meal as occasion for
poetry. In "New England / China" Corn crafts a poem of homemaking,
running from the "buds on Mother's / Haviland china" which are
"pink, flushed with excitement / At being propped in ranks along the
plate-rail," to a meal shared only in imagination with an unnamed
"you," to a fear that the dream of domestic bliss is really "insubstantial
/ Like all dream-castles based on greed." The sonnet "Dinner Theater"
takes a lighter, wittier approach to the shared meal yet makes of it
a kind of communion in its closing couplet: "And now the attentive,
worn-out Napkins, who move / Toward lips whose service, too, re-
sembles love." That Corn extends the penultimate line into hexameter
emphasizes all the more the weariness and thus the virtue of the
attentiveness, adding ethical weight to what would otherwise be a
fairly frivolous poem.

There is, indeed, much high seriousness embodied in Corn's virtuoso formal performance. Many of the poems touch on a spiritual
yearning, maybe even a mystical desire for God. Interestingly, Corn
often aims this yearning back into the past, a yearning for a God
who once seemed present, "Back in the scriptural forties," as he put

it in "Coals." In "St. Anthony in the Desert," the poet must sojourn
into the past as Anthony in the desert in search of God:

> To be filled with that hallowed emptiness
> The hermit sojourns in a desert cave.
> Fasting and prayer will make seclusion safe,
> his daily bread, each word the Spirit says.

Similarly, in the letter to Pinsky, "Destiny" is an "antique concept"
and yet "unavoidable." But Corn is not offering mere spiritual nostalgia. His backward yearning is complicated by a rueful awareness
of time's passing. "Mortality, box-cutter in hand, conquers all," he
says in "Window on the World." Both "What the Thunder Says"
and "Resources" convey an awareness of a fast-approaching day of
reckoning, the former poem ending with the fairly blunt statement
that "Nothing holds off the thunderstone I am it says your death."
    This *memento mori* theme adds depth and wisdom to Corn's pre-
occupation with poetic fame. If Corn understandably laments, in
"Nemo," that "Omitting's one way to have included / put poorer than
a nod, a spoken glance," he also knows, as he says in "Hadrian," that
"Ambition even vast finds its limit. / But love goes undefined." These
poems do occasionally speak of love, from eros to agape, but more
apparent throughout is the work of the virtuoso as an act of love,
the genius as a procreative force. One is tempted to use for Alfred
Corn the older English title for poet, "maker," under which the early
Renaissance poets sued for patronage. Such love is perhaps the true
mark of a great artist, as it is the mark in *The Divine Comedy* of the
divine artist, the supreme maker. If so, Alfred Corn has shown himself
well worth your patronage and mine.

Part V

I'm Over the American Homer

IT WAS AT ONE TIME a nearly universal assumption that a great people, state, or nation will inevitably produce a great poet, a Homer of their own. The Romans looked back at the accomplishments of the Greeks and asked, "Who is *our* Homer?" Enter Virgil. Medieval Christendom responded thereafter with Dante and Renaissance England with Milton. So who is the American Homer?

One frequent answer in the past has been Walt Whitman. Styling himself as an "everyman" kind of American, Whitman pioneered free verse, thus seeming to liberate himself from the restraints of the poetic tradition he inherited. He championed the common man and celebrated the vast and various landscape of a relatively young America. He exuded American individualism and earthy roughness. He wrote two great elegies for President Lincoln. In short, he made a direct bid to become America's poet, and America loved him for it, at first despite and eventually because of his scandalous sexual predilections. School children memorized "O Captain! My Captain!" There are high schools named after him. His verse has shown up in popular movies such as *Dead Poets Society,* and his magnum opus *Leaves of Grass* featured in a pivotal moment on *Breaking Bad.* America has loved Whitman as much or more than any poet.

I am, however, falling out of love with Whitman.

Once, I was all in on the poet. I still have a copy of *Leaves of*

Grass that my parents inscribed to me for Christmas when I was sixteen. It was my constant companion through high school and college. I read it in class when there was little else to do in my rural high school. When home from college in the summers, I carried the book into the woods behind my house and sat reading for hours while, though it pains me to admit it, smoking a corncob pipe. I recited Whitman at open-mic nights and wrote my own sprawling verse in imitation of his. I read from the poet's "Song of the Open Road" at my father's funeral. I was once enchanted with the work and the persona of Walt Whitman, but now I am becoming decidedly disenchanted.

In large part, it is teaching Whitman's work that has spoiled him for me. Not simply because teaching a work well obliges one to reread it year after year. I was constantly reading Whitman already, and returning to other authors, Dante for instance, has only strengthened my love for them. No, rather it was precisely because I was charged with explicating Whitman to young people that I began to see his luster fade. He seemed, frankly, to be telling the undergraduates all the wrong things. I'm not talking about sex. Or at least I'm not talking *just* about sex. I'm talking about his tendency to espouse and celebrate things that just aren't so.

Teaching at a small liberal arts college, I have to put a lot of time and work into convincing my students that books, particularly old books, are well worth reading. Whitman tends to tell them otherwise. In "Song of Myself," the central poem of *Leaves of Grass*, he says in one long and flowing line, "You shall no longer take things at second or third hand, nor look through the eyes of the dead, nor feed on the spectres in books." This line sounds refreshingly modern and boldly confident, but looking through the eyes of the dead is precisely what I spend a good deal of time trying to convince my students to do. I want my students to understand that if they rely upon only the intellectual fashions of the moment or only their own intuitions, they are sure to miss out on much that is true and good and beautiful. But seeing through the eyes of the dead takes work. It takes hours of reading. It might even require learning a dead language or two. Whitman offers students a seductively easy answer in the face of that hard work. You already know all you need to know, he tells them. "All truths wait in all things," he says in "Song of Myself." So, you know, why try too hard?

This attitude leads Whitman to a pronounced anti-intellectualism, as in the famous poem "When I Heard the Learn'd Astronomer," a lovely poem in its way but one that encourages the laziest habits of mind. The poem begins with the poet sitting in a lecture hall listening to an explanation of the astronomer's "charts and diagrams." Soon, however, like an undergrad grudgingly fulfilling his science gen-ed requirement, the poet grows unbearably bored. Eventually he gets up—seemingly while the lecturer is still explaining the workings of the heavens—and wanders out into "the mystical moist night-air" where he implies he learns much more than those inside the lecture hall simply by looking "up in perfect silence at the stars." I would and in fact do ardently implore my students to spend as much time as possible gazing in wonder at the night sky. To do so inevitably enriches one's soul. It helps instill a sense of wonder and a sense of proportion. But I would never juxtapose such enrichment to the other kind of enrichment that comes from actual knowledge of astronomy. Galileo famously said that "mathematics is the language in which God writes the universe." Is there not an experience of wonder to be found in learning to read that language as well as in simply gazing at the sky? Whitman gives easy permission to dismiss so much that is worth working for. To love creation, you don't need anything that is not already inside you, he says. That's not enchantment; that's just egotism in mystical dress.

Once I began considering his dismissive attitude about the wis-

dom of the ages and the spirit of inquiry, the luster began to fade
from Whitman's innovations in "free verse" as well. His poetry has
an undeniable energy which still draws me to it, but that energy is,
to a great extent, created by burning down the traditions of meter
and form that had been inseparable from the creation of verse in
English since at least Chaucer. There's a jolt of energy in that destructive act, but what others manage to do within the limits of
tradition now seems more impressive to me than what can be done
simply by ignoring all constraint. As the Irish poet Paul Muldoon
once said, "Form is a straitjacket like a straitjacket is a straitjacket to
Houdini." For all its energy, Whitman's verse sometimes does seem
like, to borrow Robert Frost's quip about free verse, "playing tennis
with the net down."

Whitman's take on religion is even worse than his take on verse.
He seems to be the voice of much that is silly and self-serving in
American spirituality, an ancestor to every self-satisfied social media profile proclaiming its owner to be "spiritual but not religious."
Whitman, of course, found inspiration for his hollow, tautological
spirituality among the American transcendentalists, those great
forerunners of vaguely comforting feelings about eschatology and
requests for "good vibrations" and "positive thoughts." Whitman's
contribution is to give the thought of Emerson an easy mass appeal.
Whitman is certainly no mere materialist, but the spiritual assertions
of "Song of Myself" don't provide a very clear sense of what he does
believe: "I am not an earth nor an adjunct of an earth, / I am the
mate and companion of people, all just as immortal and fathomless
as myself, / (They do not know how immortal, but I know.)" Such a
statement lacks the whole comfort of traditional faith but also the
courage of overt disbelief. If one can't have the confident joy of a
Dante, one could at least have the frank despair of a Samuel Beckett.
Whitman offers a spirituality that asks nothing of us but to be us.

"Why should I pray? why should I venerate and be ceremonious?" he asks in "Song of Myself." There is neither rigor nor sanctification nor awe nor sincere hope in such an untroubling spirituality. But in its ease such a "faith" has mass appeal. It asks you to bow before nothing that is not already you.

And that brings me to my real contention with Whitman: both Whitman's antagonism to tradition and his easy spirituality are rooted in the impulse to make the self the locus of all meaning. "I celebrate myself, and sing myself," begins "Song of Myself," a mantra suitable for the age of Instagram. Later in the poem he proclaims, "One world is aware and by far the largest to me, and that is myself[.]" This sense of a self so limitless it subsumes all other things under it or absorbs all other things into it is a major tributary of the great river of insanities in American life today, from the right's inability to dismiss bizarre conspiracy theories as outside the pale of probability to the left's obsession with dismissing the biological basis of gender. In Whitman we find eloquent and forceful expression of the unlimited sense of self that drives us to abandon the communities that have nourished us, to shutter the institutions that have formed us, and to shake off the marriages to which we have committed. Whitman speaks for much of America in his insistence that the limitless self is beyond fact and fiction as surely as Nietzsche's *Übermensch* is beyond good and evil. Famously the poet proclaims, "Do I contradict myself? / Very well then I contradict myself. / (I am large, I contain multitudes.)" When one is limitless, one need not bother with consistency, integrity, or reason. This is the spirit that presides over our media, social and anti-social alike. This proclamation of the limitless self is a message my students are steeped in day and night. They hear it from advertisers who see the limitless self as a limitless consumer, as well as from the empowering messages of podcasters and politicians. Sadly, those who insist there is no greatness other than your own like to think that they are inviting you out from the airless marble tombs of thought into a robust life of fresh air and sunshine in the open fields of democracy. They are, rather, calling you down from the clean air of the mountaintops to breathe the stuffy air of the closed-off self.

One good definition of an epic poem is "the story of all things," a phrase Samuel Barrow applied to Milton's *Paradise Lost* but which could also be said, from the perspective of the culture which produced it, of the *Iliad*, the *Aeneid,* and the *Divine Comedy*. *Leaves of Grass* is also meant to offer "the story of all things," but, despite its laudable attention to all the varied landscapes and human occupations of young America, in Whitman's poetry the self *is* all things. Everything is subsumed under the glorious identity of the autonomous individual. My students are constantly told this story. It is in the air all around them. I want the books we read to offer them a different and a better and a truer story, one which gives them an opportunity to be a part of something bigger than all of us. I want great books to call them to an encounter with the *givenness* of the world rather than just with an infinitely malleable and all-consuming self at the center of all things.

I'm not "canceling" Whitman. I will continue to teach his work and to pick up *Leaves of Grass* from time to time simply for the pleasure of reading it. I will continue to teach Whitman because, despite his own anti-traditionalism, he has come to occupy an important place in the American literary tradition. He also offers an interesting entryway into discussion of American optimism and individualism, a useful window on social and intellectual history. More importantly, I will continue to teach and read Whitman because there is much that is beautiful in his verse. "When Lilacs Last in the Dooryard Bloom'd" achieves an almost classical dignity and solemnity at times in its lament for Lincoln. Throughout "Song of Myself" and in other poems such as "I Hear America Singing," "Crossing Brooklyn Ferry," and "Out of the Cradle Endlessly Rocking," there are many finely envisioned images, pictures of rugged honest labor, of everyday American life, and of natural beauty. It is sometimes worth wading through Whitman's self-importance and eyeroll-inducing enthusiasms to see the world through his eyes, which are now too "the eyes of the dead."

No, I'm not canceling Whitman. But my own enthusiasm for his poetry is waning. The poet whose daring versification and daring lifestyle were once seen as the epitome of counter-culture has come to seem to me all too mainstream, the very voice of an age of superficial egotism.

A Disgusting Poem about
God's Goodness

"THIS POEM IS DISGUSTING," one of my students declared not long ago as we settled in for a discussion of the *Inferno*, the first part of Dante's *Divine Comedy*. She wasn't wrong. Writing in the early fourteenth century, the exiled Florentine soldier, public servant, and poet Dante Alighieri vividly depicts the horrors of Hell as he imagined them: gluttons prone in the mud and feeding on filth; heretics cleaved from head to belly button as they walk; a traitor frozen in ice up to the neck and gnawing on the head of a fellow sinner. Disgusting? Absolutely. But as I told my student, sin is disgusting. Throughout Dante's *Inferno* we see the human form twisted, split, tortured, and mutilated in numerous ways because Dante is determined to make the point that sin is tragic because it deforms what God has formed. Few books so viscerally convey how repugnant sin truly is, how counter it is to the ultimate beauty of God.

Central to Dante's vision is the belief that God is the creator, the only maker. Dante would no doubt agree with the words, here translated by Henry Chadwick, which Augustine addresses to God in his *Confessions*: "Without you, whatever exists would not exist." For Dante, as for Augustine, evil is not a created thing—not a thing that can be said to truly exist—but rather a corruption, a kind of rot. When God pronounces His creation "good," He is not generalizing or overlooking anything. All that He creates is good. God forms; sin deforms.

The chief example of this principle in Dante's poem is the effect of sin on the *Imago Dei*, the image of God in man. In one of the most heartbreaking moments of the poem, Dante—who is the main character in his own poem—meets in Hell his old mentor, Brunetto Latini. The poet is dismayed to find his teacher condemned to a circle of Hell set aside for sodomites. At first, however, he cannot recognize his old teacher, only gradually seeing the man God made in the wreckage caused by sin:

> And I, when he stretched out his arm to me,
>   searched his baked features closely, till at last
>   I traced his image from my memory
> in spite of the burnt crust, and bending near
>   to put my face closer to his, at last
>   I answered: "Ser Brunetto, are *you* here?"
> (*Inferno* 15.25–30)[1]

John Ciardi's translation, with its use of *image*, is perhaps closer to an interpretation than a direct translation here, as nothing like *Image* or *Imago* appears in the original Italian, and Anthony Esolen's more direct translation has Dante say only "I ... so fixed my eyes upon his crusted looks / that even the charred features could not keep / My intellect from recognizing them." Yet Ciardi's translation picks up the deeper sense: that sin has obscured the *Imago Dei* in Brunetto. In a sense, eternally committed to the sin that separates him from God, Brunetto is less Brunetto than he once was even during his sinful life. All that is "Brunetto" was made by God, but Brunetto has been tragically unmade by sin.

---

1. I quote throughout from Ciardi's translation, except where otherwise noted.

To witness this unmaking is why Dante must go through Hell before he is ready for the beatific vision. His journey is ultimately to Heaven, but the guide sent to him, the great Roman poet Virgil, first takes Dante through Hell so that he can see the terrible destructive power of sin. He must come to know sin and evil as a horrible undoing.

While Dante and Augustine saw evil and sin as a kind of nothingness, that does not mean they did not take the effects of this corruption very seriously. As Augustine argues, starvation is merely the absence of food, but that absence can destroy our bodies from the inside and kill us. To learn to take this destruction seriously enough to desire true repentance is why Dante must take the grand tour of Hell before he is given a vision of Heaven.

At several points on his journey through Hell, Dante weeps to see the deforming effects of sin on God's image in man. When he observes the soothsayers, who have had their heads twisted backwards on their bodies as retribution for their attempt to see further ahead than is granted to man, Dante writes, again in Ciardi's translation,

> Reader, so may God grant you to understand
>   my poem and profit from it, ask yourself
>   how I could check my tears, when near at hand
> I saw the image of our humanity
>   distorted so that the tears that burst from their eyes
>   ran down the cleft of their buttocks.
>
> (*Inferno* 20.19–24)

At this point in the poem, the Italian is very close to how Ciardi renders it: *la nostra imagine*, which means something like "the image of ours" and which Esolen translates as "our human image." In a similar vein of lament, after the poet witnesses the sowers of discord, who have been hacked and split as retribution for their divisiveness, Dante

says, "The sight of that parade of broken dead / had left my eyes so
sotted with their tears / I longed to stay and weep" (*Inferno* 29.1–3).
Though there are also, especially further down in Hell, those among
the damned whose crimes are so vile Dante can summon little to
no pity for them, on the balance, he has learned his lesson well. He
has learned that sin tragically unmakes what God has made good.

His brilliant guide, Virgil, is not so quick a study on this particular
matter. When Dante weeps at the sight of the mangled *Imago* in the
soothsayers, the great pagan poet chastises him for the compassion,
saying

> There is no place
> for pity here. Who is more arrogant
> within his soul, who is more impious
> than one who dares to sorrow at God's judgment?
> (*Inferno* 20.27–30)

In the poem's allegory, Virgil represents human reason, the best
man can do on common grace alone without special revelation from
God. Eventually Virgil will reach his limit, and Dante will leave
him behind to be escorted into Heaven by the beautiful Beatrice,
who represents divine revelation. In this changing of guides, Dante
reflects the assertion of Thomas Aquinas that human reason can
show us much—for instance that God exists—but some facets of the
faith—like the Trinity and the dual nature of Christ—are beyond
the ability of reason alone to demonstrate. Reason tells us that God's
judgment on sinners is just. Only revelation can tell us "The steadfast
love of the Lord never ceases; his mercies never come to an end; they
are new every morning; great is your faithfulness" (Lamentations 3:
22–23, ESV).

But the poet does not leave us with the tragedy of sin. This, after all, is a divine *comedy*, not an infernal tragedy. In part three of the great poem, the *Paradiso*, Dante again meets those he cannot recognize. Now, however, they are not unrecognizable because God's image in them has been marred but rather because it has become so much clearer than it ever was in earthly life. When, for instance, Dante meets the nun Piccarda, she says to him, "if you search your memory with care, / despite my greater beauty, you will know // I am Piccarda" (*Paradiso* 3.47–49). Dante replies, "Something inexpressibly / divine shines in your face, subliming you / beyond your image in my memory" (3.58–60). She is now more Piccarda than she ever was before her death. Indeed, it is only after he has himself been sanctified and made ready for Heaven that Dante's own name appears in the poem, atop Mt. Purgatory as he prepares to journey into Heaven. Sin's deformity repaired, he becomes the Dante God made, a bearer of God's holy image.

In the final beatific vision at the end of the poem, we see the *Imago Dei* made perfect in Christ's human form ascended into Heaven. I will quote it at length to give a sense of the glorious Trinitarian splendor in which the *Imago* now appears:

> Within the depthless deep and clear existence
>   of that abyss of light three circles shone—
>   three in color, one in circumference:
> the second from the first, rainbow from rainbow;
>   the third, an exhalation of pure fire
>   equally breathed forth by the other two.
> But oh how much my words miss my conception,
>   which is itself so far from what I saw
>   that to call it feeble would be rank deception!
> O Light Eternal fixed in Itself alone,
>   by itself understood, which from Itself
>   loves and glows, self-knowing and self-known;

that second aureole which shone forth in Thee,
    conceived as a reflection of the first—
    or which appeared so to my scrutiny—
seemed in Itself of Its own coloration
    to be painted with man's image. I fixed by eyes
    on that alone in rapturous contemplation.

(*Paradiso* 33.115–132)

This is Dante's vision, nearly the final of the poem, of Christ as all that man was created to be and more. We see the Image of God in perfection and in perfect glory, and the ugliness of sin, which we had to remember in order to get here, fades from memory as true reality is glimpsed for the first time.

Like *Pinocchio*, the *Divine Comedy* is a story about how to become a real boy. But in order to appreciate that coming into being to which Dante is called by his Creator, he must first witness the horrifying effects of sin as it eats at God's good creation. The poem is disgusting, indeed. And disgusted we ought to be. We must always remember, however, that if we are willing to honestly access the repulsiveness of our sin, a greater beauty than we could ever imagine awaits us.

Hamlet and the *Memento Mori* Tradition

Do you remember that scene in *The Princess Bride* when the Man in Black challenges Vizzini to the contest of the poisoned cup? Vizzini must determine which of two cups is poisoned, and then they will both drink. At one point Vizzini says to the Man in Black:

> You've beaten my giant, which means you're exceptionally strong. So, you could have put the poison in your own goblet, trusting on your strength to save you. So I can clearly not choose the wine in front of you. But, you've also bested my Spaniard which means you must have studied. And in studying, you must have learned that man is mortal, so you would have put the poison as far from yourself as possible, so I can clearly not choose the wine in front of me!

Apparently, a classical education is good preparation for a career as the Dread Pirate Roberts.

Indeed, generations of dialectic students have been introduced to reason via the classic syllogism that goes: Man is mortal; Socrates is man; therefore Socrates is mortal. Nonetheless, it seems it is always hard for us to put ourselves in Socrates' place. Through a constant effort, usually invisible to ourselves, we manage to delude ourselves into thinking we are immortal. We distract ourselves from death. Until, that is, great literature comes along and dispels the delusion.

In act 5, scene 1 of *Hamlet*, Hamlet and Horatio famously encounter a gravedigger who has just dug up the remains of a court
jester, Yorick, whom Hamlet had apparently known in his youth.
Hamlet takes up the skull of the dead jester and delivers one of his
most famous speeches:

> Alas, poor Yorick! I knew him, Horatio; a fellow of infinite
> jest, of most excellent fancy; he hath borne me on his back a
> thousand times; and now, how abhorred in my imagination it
> is! My gorge rises at it. Here hung those lips that I have kissed
> I know not how oft. Where be your gibes now? Your gambols?
> Your songs? Your flashes of merriment, that were wont to set
> the table on a roar? Not one now, to mock your own grinning?
> Quite chop-fallen? Now get you to my lady's chamber, and tell
> her, let her paint an inch thick, to this favor she must come.

Looking on the skull of Yorick, Hamlet reflects that man—all men—
are mortal. Though the court jester distracts us with merriment and
the court beauty distracts us with makeup, there is always the skull
underneath. Death always waits in the wings. Hamlet continues:

> To what base uses we may return, Horatio! Why may not imag-
> ination trace the noble dust of Alexander, till he find it stopping
> a bung-hole?

Horatio attempts to brush off the suggestion that Alexander the
Great may be found these days plugging a hole in a beer barrel by
suggesting that it is "too curious" to think so. Hamlet replies:

No, faith, not a jot; but to follow him thither with modesty
enough and likelihood to lead it; as thus: Alexander died,
Alexander was buried, Alexander returneth into dust, the dust
is earth, of earth we make loam, and why of that loam whereto
he was converted might they not stop a beer-barrel?

> Imperial Caesar, dead and turn'd to clay,
> Might stop a hole to keep the wind away.
> O, that that earth, which kept the world in awe,
> Should patch a wall to expel the winter's flaw!

In making this point, Hamlet echoes the famous words of the funeral
service from the Book of Common Prayer: "Earth to earth, ashes
to ashes, dust to dust," which in turn is an echo of Ecclesiastes 3:20:
"All go unto one place; all are of the dust, and all turn to dust again."
It is also an echo of Genesis 3:19: "You are dust and to dust you shall
return." The melancholy Dane has joined a long line of Christian
writers, preachers, and artists imploring the Christian toward *memento
mori*, that is to remember the ever-present fact of death.

The sober recognition that man is mortal is, of course, an important
part of the literary tradition long before the Christian age. When
Glaucus and Diomedes meet in battle in book 6 of Homer's *Iliad*,
Glaucus says, in Stanley Lombardo's translation,

> "Human generations are like leaves in their seasons.
> The wind blows them to the ground, but the tree
> Sprouts new ones when spring comes again.
> Men too. Their generations come and go."

This poignant reminder of the transience of life comes not in spite
of the heroic warrior culture about which Homer writes but rather

because of it. Those who make their lives by daily risking death have no delusions of immortality. Think of the Sioux of the American plains riding into battle with the mantra: "Today is a good day to die."

The simile of the leaves from the *Iliad* shows up again in book 6 of Virgil's *Aeneid*, as Aeneas arrives in the underworld. Virgil writes, as again translated by Lombardo:

> And now a whole crowd rushed streaming
> To the banks, mothers and husbands, bodies
> Of high-souled heroes finished with life,
> Boys and unwed girls, and young men
> Placed upon the pyre before their parents' eyes.
> As many as leaves that fall in the woods
> At autumn's first frost, as many as birds
> That teem to shore when the cold year
> Drives them over the sea to sunny lands.

Virgil suggests, as did Homer in the underworld passages of the *Odyssey*, that death comes for all manner of human beings. A similar reminder was given to conquering Roman leaders as they paraded in triumph through Rome, a slave supposedly standing behind them in the chariot to whisper "remember you will die": *memento mori*.

This ancient pagan awareness of death received a strong second from the Christian Church. The acceptance of mortality is, of course, a necessary condition for the emphasis on resurrection that is at the heart of the Christian faith. In the Old Testament, Ecclesiastes, naturally, emphasizes human finiteness and thus the inevitability of death. It is joined by the Psalms, where we read in Psalm 103:

> As for man, his days are like grass—
> he blooms like a flower of the field;

when the wind passes over, it vanishes,
and its place remembers it no more.

The sentiment is repeated in the New Testament in 1 Peter 1:24:

For "All flesh is like grass,
and all its glory like a flower of the grass.
The grass withers, and the flower falls."

The church has known from the beginning that, if we are to rightly
value the offer of eternal life in Christ, we must take seriously the
certainty of death. In doing so, we shape our hopes and hearts toward
eternity. As the Psalms also say, in Psalm 39, "Lord, let me know
my end, and the measure of my days; let me know how fleeting my
life is!" This is why Christians traditionally receive the ashes upon
our head on Ash Wednesday and are reminded that "we are but the
dust": *memento mori*.

Accordingly, one of Christianity's greatest minds, Augustine of
Hippo, tells in his *Confessions* of a friend's death and follows up the
account with this prayer and meditation:

O God of hosts, turn us and show us your face, and we shall be
safe. For wherever the human soul turns itself other than you,
it is fixed in sorrows, even if it is fixed upon beautiful things
external to you and external to itself, which would nevertheless
be nothing if they did not have their being from you. Things
rise and set: in their emerging they begin as it were to be, and
grow to perfection; having reached perfection, they grow old
and die. Not everything grows old, but everything dies. So when
things rise and emerge into existence, the faster they grow to
be, the quicker they rush towards non-being.

Augustine's understanding of God as perfect, uncreated being gives him a solid understanding that we are made of something else, something that is less permanent.

As Christianity spread north in the early Middle Ages to take root among the Germanic peoples of Northern Europe, the Biblical insistence on man's mortality found a partner in the Germanic culture's view of all things as transient. Like the Homeric heroes before them, warrior peoples like the Anglo-Saxons who conquered much of the British Isles had a practical understanding of the fragility of human life. This blending of Christian *memento mori* with the Germanic sense of fatalism led to fine poetry. In the Old-English poem known as "The Wanderer" a lone survivor of a defeated warband laments the inevitable passing of all things. Here is a passage from A.S. Kline's translation:

> The wise man must see,
> How all will be ghastly,
> When all the weal of this
> World lies wasted,
> As now here and there
> Over this middle-earth,
> Wind-beaten
> The walls stand
> Rime be-frosted,
> Buildings storm-swept.
> The halls are broken,
> Warrior lords lie
> Bereft of delight.
> Fallen the throng,
> Proud by the wall.
> Some war wasted,

Ferried on their way,
Him the bird took
Beyond the deep seas,
Him the grey wolf
Garnered for death,
Him all dreary
Man hid in an
Earthly grave.

Wisdom is linked by the poet with the awareness of death's ubiquity and inevitability. There are numerous ways to die, and everyone will get a turn in this world of transience. Later in the poem he adds this:

Where is the horse now?
Where is the rider?
Where is the gold-giver?
Where is the seat at the gathering?
Where now are the feasts in the halls?
Alas for the gleaming cup!
Alas the mailed warrior!
Alas for the prince's pride!
How that age has passed,
Dark under night-helm,
As though it never were!

There is a world-weary humility in these lines that reminds us that we are utterly dependent on a Being beyond our limited being, that we are fleeting.

The most famous of the Old-English poems is *Beowulf*, and it too contains a substantial amount of *memento mori*. Early in the poem, using the understatement that is such a prominent part of Anglo-

Saxon poetics, the narrator says, as translated by the great Irish poet
Seamus Heaney,

> Death is not easily
> Escaped from by anyone:
> All of us with souls, earth-dwellers
> And children of men, must make our way
> To a destination already ordained
> Where the body, after the banqueting,
> Sleeps on its deathbed.

Later, after Beowulf has defeated both the demon-monster Grendel
and the monster's even more hideous mother, the hero is both con-
gratulated and warned by the wise king Hrothgar. Hrothgar tells
Beowulf a parable about a powerful warrior who grows arrogant.
The wise king says,

> Then finally the end arrives
> When the body he was lent collapses and falls
> Prey to its death; ancestral possessions
> And the goods he hoarded are inherited by another
> Who lets them go with a liberal hand.

He ends his speech by enumerating the possibilities for death:

> For a brief while your strength is in bloom
> But it fades quickly; and soon there will follow
> Illness or the sword to lay you low,
> Or a sudden fire or surge of water
> Or jabbing blade or javelin from the air
> Or repellent age. Your piercing eye

Will dim and darken; and death will arrive,
Dear warrior, to sweep you away.

There are numerous ways to die. One may think that Hrothgar
seems to have missed his calling as an insurance actuary, but there
is a very important point being made for the benefit of the young
warrior at the top of his game. That point is that we're all going to
die. *Memento mori.*

By the high Middle Ages, the *memento mori* had become a prominent part of Christian spirituality in the West. In canto 3 of the
Inferno, Dante takes up the simile of the leaves from Homer and
Virgil to describe the damned responding to the call of the ferryman
of the dead. Here is John Ciardi's very accessible translation:

As leaves in autumn loosen and stream down
    until the branch stands bare above its tatters
    spread on the rustling ground, so one by one

the evil seed of Adam in its Fall
    cast themselves, at his signal from the shore
    and streamed away like birds who hear their call.

Dante's simile is directly modeled on Virgil's version, but Dante adds
the Christian understanding of the fall of man as the initial entrance
of death into the world. The falling leaves become fallen souls, and
we are encouraged to think about our ultimate destination.

In the late Middle Ages, the Black Death (or bubonic plague),
along with the Hundred Years War, famine, and other apocalyptic
events, pushed *memento mori* into the forefront of Christian culture.
One would not be surprised to find a human skull among the books
and papers of a scholar's chambers. The nobility paid handsomely

for burial in a cadaver tomb, a sepulcher topped with a sculpture of a skeleton or decomposing body to represent the remains entombed inside. This period sees the rise of the figure we sometimes call the Grim Reaper, or just "death" in popular art. The *Danse Macabre*, an image of a dancing Death leading to the grave persons from all walks of life, became common as murals in cemeteries and even on the walls of churches. Hans Holbein the Younger's drawings of this motif were published from woodcuts and became extremely popular throughout Europe. In the late medieval morality play *Everyman*, the title character—who is really all of us—is suddenly surprised by a personified death as he goes about his business. In Chaucer's *Pardoner's Tale,* three men go seeking death in order to kill him, but find death instead in the form of an ill-gotten treasure. *Memento mori* is ubiquitous at the close of the Middle Ages.

The *memento mori* tradition is not smothered by the new learning we call the Renaissance, but, rather, flourishes in the sixteenth and seventeenth centuries. Among the most famous Renaissance literary *memento mori* is the seventeenth of John Donne's *Devotions Upon Emergent Occasions*, which begins with the epigraph "Now this bell tolling softly for another, says to me, Thou must die" and which includes the famous phrase "never send to know for whom the bell tolls; it tolls for thee." There are elements of the *memento mori* tradition to be found in Edmund Spenser's great Renaissance epic romance *The Faerie Queene* and even in Milton's *Paradise Lost*. But the best-known example from the period is certainly Shakespeare's Hamlet pondering the skull of Yorick.

Though modernity's sometimes unquestioning faith in progress and the supposedly unlimited potential of man pushed, even within the church, the *memento mori* topos into the background, the tradition still has its spokesmen in the modern world. Both Tennyson's *Idylls of the King* and his *In Memoriam* contain strong elements of *memento mori.* There may even be a hint of the *memento mori* in Robert Frost's assertion that "Nothing Gold Can Stay."

Perhaps my favorite example of the *memento mori* topos from the modern age is Gerard Manley Hopkins's poem "Spring and Fall." Hopkins addresses the poem to a young child, but he is clearly speaking to all of us:

> Márgarét, áre you gríeving
> Over Goldengrove unleaving?
> Leáves, like the things of man, you
> With your fresh thoughts care for, can you?
> Ah! ás the heart grows older
> It will come to such sights colder
> By and by, nor spare a sigh
> Though worlds of wanwood leafmeal lie;
> And yet you wíll weep and know why.
> Now no matter, child, the name:
> Sórrow's spríngs áre the same.
> Nor mouth had, no nor mind, expressed
> What heart heard of, ghost guessed:
> It ís the blight man was born for,
> It is Margaret you mourn for.

Like Frost later, Hopkins reminds us that nature itself offers a version of *memento mori* in the inevitable changing of the seasons. He asserts the wisdom of accepting this knowledge while at the same time acknowledging our inner revolt against the regime of death. This is the true point of the reminder of our death: that we would not put our hopes in this life lasting and thus would fix our hope on an eternal life. We accept death in order to enter into its final defeat.

I think these reminders from the past are a useful antidote to all the things today which serve to distract us from our own mortality. Although we in one sense certainly live in a "culture of death," it seems to be primarily a culture of someone else's death. We find myriad ways to delude ourselves into thinking we are immortal. The great tradition's motif of *memento mori* calls us to a kind of humility and to a seriousness about what really lasts. Psalm 90 says "Teach us to number our days, that we may gain a heart of wisdom." Alas Poor Yorick. We are all Yorick. It is ourselves we mourn for.

Don't Quit Your Day Job

WIMP WAS THE COLOGNE "for the man who doesn't ride a horse." At least, that is what the label said. Unfortunately, most of the men who don't ride horses also didn't buy *Wimp* cologne. Nevertheless, my parents tried. That was what they did: try. They had printed up numerous rolls of labels with the brand name and the tag line, "for the man who doesn't ride a horse," and they spent evening after evening pouring rubbing alcohol and a proprietary blend of scent additives into tiny jars onto which to affix the little labels of fake gold foil. They visited every drugstore and five and dime in central Oklahoma, smilingly reassuring bemused managers that *Wimp* was no joke, or not entirely a joke anyway. As it turns out, however, men who don't ride horses generally aspire to smell like men who do. Production of *Wimp* ceased within a couple of months. After the endeavor fizzled out, we were left with countless rolls of the shiny gold foil labels. For years, we used them instead of tape, rolling the labels into little sticky tubes to affix pictures into scrapbooks or to make school art projects adhere.

I was raised by writers. They were serious artists, but they were also often seriously underfunded. My mom was a middle school English teacher, and my dad generally took whatever work he could find until he eventually settled into working for the state Employment Security Commission. Still, like most writers, they were always looking for a better way to support themselves—and their three children—while freeing up time and energy to write. Like most writers, they were dreamers.

Of course, plenty of great writers have had memorable day jobs. Shakespeare acted in his plays and was part owner and operator of the theatre company. T.S. Eliot worked first in a bank and later in publishing. Toni Morrison also worked in publishing for many years. William Carlos Williams was a physician, and Wallace Stevens was an insurance executive. More recently, Ted Kooser also had a long career in insurance. At one point along the way, Kurt Vonnegut managed a Saab dealership. My parents did what they could.

By the time I was a small child, my parents had tried several businesses, including a shoe store, a restaurant, and a junk shop. The restaurant was in the back of the shoe store, an apparent effort to save a struggling business by adding another struggling business to the back room. Small town Oklahoma apparently didn't want more food and didn't need more shoes. The junk shop, however, was promising. I can just barely remember it, a paradise for a small boy. There were shelves of old glassware, casting streaks of blue and green light on the bare wooden floor. There were old toasters, record players, and small appliances. I was once allowed to bring home from the shop a model train engine, with no tracks to run it on. This marvelous place, however, was not profitable enough to support the family, so it was back to the regular work for Mom and Dad.

Teaching was always steady, if irritating and not highly lucrative, work for Mom. My father, however, had a harder time finding steady employment. For a short but glorious while, he managed the local Sonic Drive-In, and I can vividly remember the vanilla ice cream cone I got when we visited him at work one night. Most of the time in my early years, he worked odd jobs such as painting houses or hauling away junk. When I got a little older, I sometimes went with him to scrape old paint before he put on the new coat or to help load smaller chunks of refuse into the back of my grandfather's old truck, which we used for the hauling. Watching my father the poet, my father the intellectual, climb a ladder to touch up the lattice work on a crumbling Victorian or drag charred lumber out of a burned-out trailer to be loaded on the truck, I absorbed an important lesson about the true ratio between high ambition and hard reality. I learned about sacrifice, love, and grit.

I learned the same lesson from my mother's years teaching school. It was work she excelled at, and it was work she loved, I think, in a way. She knew that what she did for a living made a difference, and she put her heart and soul into the work. Still, she would have preferred to have been writing instead of planning lessons and grading the compositions of eighth graders. The pay was low. The work was difficult, thanks especially to certain kids and certain parents. Still, for decades, she taught kids in small town Oklahoma how to diagram sentences and to memorize "Annabel Lee." Her own children she, too, taught about sacrifice, love, and grit.

My parents did what they had to do, and they kept dreaming. In the meantime, I watched and learned. From *Wimp* and similar ventures, I learned how to dream and how to take the necessary steps toward that dream, even when it meant walking out over the cliff like Wile E. Coyote. The restaurant, the shoes, the junk, and the cologne didn't work out, but my parents kept working at it. In a world that demanded demanding work from them, they kept their eyes open for a way to give more time to art, even while they worked hard at more regular jobs with integrity and purpose. They got up every morning and did what they had to do, and part of what they had to do was the art they were called to create. Witnessing that dedication on both sides of the equation—sticking with the art and doing what was necessary to feed the family—shaped the way my life would be, shaped my own relationship to my art and to my responsibilities. I probably wouldn't be a writer without some spark I inherited from them, something in the DNA. I definitely wouldn't be a writer—or a decent father—without the example of their dedication and determination.

In addition to being a hard worker, my father was a charmer. From him I also learned how to talk my way into opportunities, an invaluable skill for a writer. He might not have been able to convince many pharmacists to stock the cologne for wimps, but he was able to talk his way into a lot of other good things. He managed to turn a short-term gig taking tolls at the turnpike gate into a long-term employment for the state, ironically helping other people find jobs for the Oklahoma Employment Security Commission. My father spent a little bit of time in the Air Force before he married my mother, and at his new job with the state, he quickly developed a specialty of working with veterans and started teaching them poetry and creative writing as a means of coping with trauma. That led to a job with the VA as a vet's rep. On top of that, drawing on this literary experience, he was able to talk his way into several assignments as an editor, putting together a couple of important books about the bombing of the Murrah Federal Building. He wasn't talking his way into things beyond his reach; he did these jobs well. He was, however, talking his way into opportunities beyond what would normally be given to someone without credentials and pedigree. This is something most artists must learn to do, and it has served me well at times.

My mother's determination paid off in a long career as a novelist. An author of many novels for young readers, she was inducted into the Oklahoma Writers Hall of Fame in 2013. It has been a great joy watching her success as a novelist, which began with the publication of her first book, *Red-Dirt Jessie,* just as I was about to graduate from high school. But more valuable than watching her win was watching her work toward the victory. She taught generations of kids in rural Oklahoma to write, to read, and to think. She attended every school play, choir concert, and band performance in which her three children were involved. And she kept writing. Whether it was on a Sunday afternoon or after dinner while the rest of the family watched TV, she found the time for the art to which she was called. That example, more than any gifts in the DNA, accounts for any success I have as a writer.

When I think about those little bottles of cheap cologne, I think about a couple of people trying to find a way to both make art and love well the people they were given to care for. We didn't have all the luxuries and the trendiest clothing while I was growing up, but we had plenty to eat and a roof over our heads. My dad may have had to patch that roof himself as best he could, but we were safe and dry. There is an idea that circulates in artistic circles that an artist has to give up everything for artistic success, that one cannot love well both the art and the people given to one by life's circumstances. The lives of many writers I greatly admire—Charles Dickens, W.B. Yeats, Sylvia Plath, John Berryman—would seem to offer evidence for that idea, but my parents proved it wrong. Ask me what real success smells like, and I will tell you it smells like *Wimp*.

A Little Homily on Providence

At the end of John Milton's *Paradise Lost*, as Adam and Eve are being expelled from Eden, Milton writes:

> Som natural tears they drop'd, but wip'd them soon;
> The World was all before them, where to choose
> Thir place of rest, and Providence thir guide:
> They hand in hand with wandring steps and slow,
> Through *Eden* took thir solitarie way.

Milton imagines the scene in a way that suggests Adam and Eve take two powerful consolations with them from the garden. The first is marriage ("hand in hand" they go), a moving suggestion that married companionship is a little remnant of Paradise left in the fallen world. The other thing they take with them is an even greater comfort: the promise of redemption in Christ that has been given through the prophecy that the seed of the woman will crush the head of the serpent. Milton, having shown the long unfolding of history that will lead up to and center on the birth, death, and resurrection of Christ, refers to this promise, and the promise of companionship in marriage, as "Providence" and tells us that it will be their guide. In other words, *Paradise Lost* has a happy ending. Adam and Eve are not alone. God is in control.

Some ancient writers took a strongly deterministic view of reality. Stoics like Marcus Aurelius asserted that everything that happens has to happen, that it perhaps even happens the same way over and over again infinitely in a loop of "eternal recurrence," though his emphasis on moral responsibility seems, thankfully, to contradict his determinism. Some modern writers, like the novelist Thomas Hardy, take an even bleaker view of free will, asserting that our entire lives are ruled by an impersonal and unbending fate established by biology and/or our social circumstances. Other writers, particularly modern existentialists like Jean-Paul Sartre, have asserted that, on the contrary, we are completely and absolutely and terrifyingly free, with no power, personal or impersonal, above us in the cosmos. For these writers, life is completely meaningless, and we all must make up our own meaning for it. For the existentialist, that meaning can be whatever we have the desire and strength to make it.

So the options available at this point in the history of thought often seem to be a grim and iron determinism on the one hand and a senseless and absurd aimlessness on the other: either a deep rut or no road at all. But the Christian concept of Providence avoids both of these depressing views of human agency. Providence is neither iron fate nor meaningless meandering. Providence is, most simply, where God's absolute sovereignty meets God's perfect love.

Not surprisingly, Scripture frequently calls us out of anxiousness and into the comfort of God's Providence. In Romans 8:27–32 we read:

> And he who searches hearts knows what is the mind of the Spirit, because the Spirit intercedes for the saints according to the will of God. And we know that for those who love God all things work together for good, for those who are called according to his purpose. For those whom he foreknew he also

predestined to be conformed to the image of his Son, in order
that he might be the firstborn among many brothers. And those
whom he predestined he also called, and those whom he called
he also justified, and those whom he justified he also glorified.

What then shall we say to these things? If God is for us, who
can be against us? He who did not spare his own Son but gave
him up for us all, how will he not also with him graciously give
us all things?

Paul paints a picture of a loving God lovingly orchestrating all things
for our good. But we have to be careful not to read this reductively.
We have to remember that some of the saints whom God is working
all things for the good of have died at the hands of persecutors, as
Paul surely did himself. We have to remember that other saints for
whom God has worked all things to good have suffered in myriad
other ways. The saints for whom all things are worked for good have
died in car crashes and from cancer. They have lost jobs, incomes,
and, even worse, have lost loved ones. They have been brought low
by the struggles of life. What God's Providence clearly cannot mean
is that we will always get the cheerful lives and worldly "success"
that we crave. We have to understand that trusting in Providence
means being truly hopeful, not merely optimistic. We are not merely
waiting on things to "go our way." We are waiting on the ultimate
redemption of God's creation. We seek a city that is beyond this
world as we know it.

Living with this promise of redemption means living now with
the given. That is, living with a sense of the "givenness" of life. This
goes against the grain of our modern assumptions. We are all now
by default Henry David Thoreau who declared, "Know all men by
these presents, that I, Henry Thoreau, do not wish to be regarded as

a member of any incorporated society which I have not joined." But that is not how God's Providence works. The communities He plants us in, the husbands or wives He gives us, the liberal arts education He provides us, the neighbors, the business associates, the aches and pains, the chores and care for others: all of it is part of His redemptive work, the givenness, His Providence. We must be good stewards and take responsibility, but we should not be so quick to assume we are the masters of our own lives. We are most free when we are not under the illusion that we are in control, because only then are we freed from the anxieties of self-ownership, as my colleague Alan Noble has pointed out in his book *You Are Not Your Own*. Jesus speaks of this freedom in Matthew, chapter 6:

> "Therefore I tell you, do not be anxious about your life, what you will eat or what you will drink, nor about your body, what you will put on. Is not life more than food, and the body more than clothing? Look at the birds of the air: they neither sow nor reap nor gather into barns, and yet your heavenly Father feeds them. Are you not of more value than they? And which of you by being anxious can add a single hour to his span of life? And why are you anxious about clothing? Consider the lilies of the field, how they grow: they neither toil nor spin, yet I tell you, even Solomon in all his glory was not arrayed like one of these. But if God so clothes the grass of the field, which today is alive and tomorrow is thrown into the oven, will he not much more clothe you, O you of little faith? Therefore do not be anxious, saying, 'What shall we eat?' or 'What shall we drink?' or 'What shall we wear?' For the Gentiles seek after all these things, and your heavenly Father knows that you need them all. But seek

first the kingdom of God and his righteousness, and all these
things will be added to you.

"Therefore do not be anxious about tomorrow, for tomorrow will
be anxious for itself. Sufficient for the day is its own trouble."

Do not miss the note at the end. There will be trouble, sufficient
trouble for today. Biblically, Providence is found paired with suffering
and trouble. God's Providence is not a promise of immediate happy
results and your best life now. It is a promise that there is an ultimate
good ending in the final redemption. There is a plan you can trust
even as things around you seem to go up in flames. The little dog
with the coffee cup is actually right: this truly is fine. Between the
utter determinism of some and the total self-ownership of others is
the ideal of Providence, the place where God's absolute sovereignty
meets his absolute love: We are neither ruled by an iron fate nor left
to our own plans. We are, rather, cared for.

I want to end by pointing you to a poem I think about when I think
about suffering and God's Providence. It was written by Jane Kenyon,
one of my favorite late-twentieth-century poets, and she wrote the
poem as she was dying from cancer. It is called "Let Evening Come."
Kenyon begins in a gentle way, describing late afternoon light as it
moves through a picturesque rural setting. In a delightful simile, she
compares the beginning of cricket song in the evening to a woman
taking up her knitting needles.

So far the poem is perhaps little more than a simple reflection on
the pleasantness of the closing of the day. Yet as she continues to
develop the imagery of the poem, we come more and more to see the
unexpectedness of evening, as well as its inevitability. In other words,

this "evening" becomes more clearly metaphorical. This sense of an ending culminates, fittingly, in the poem's final stanza:

> Let it come, as it will, and don't
> be afraid. God does not leave us
> comfortless, so let evening come.

Faced with impending death from an incurable disease, Kenyon reminded herself (and us) that "God does not leave us comfortless." And that line break reminds us that our great comfort is that "God does not leave us." He has said, "I will never leave you or abandon you," hasn't He? Our God's Providence is His presence, His nearness even when evening comes.

Take heart.

Appendix

Form from Dust: An Interview with Casie Dodd

EDITOR'S NOTE: Long before starting Belle Point Press, I was a student of Dr. Ben Myers as an undergraduate; he has since remained a mentor and friend over the years. When his most recent poetry collection was published by Lamar University Literary Press in 2022, I talked with him about the book for *Whale Road Review*; the interview appeared in issue 30.

Tell us a little more about your writing and teaching background.
I've been writing poetry since I was in middle school, at least. Both of my parents were writers, so it seemed like a natural thing to do. In high school I spent two summer terms at the wonderful Oklahoma Summer Arts Institute, studying poetry with B.H. Fairchild and Ellen Kort. After getting a BA in English, I decided to pursue a PHD rather than the MFA. My reasoning was that I wanted to learn all I could about poetics and about literature (and history and philosophy). So I ended up studying the Renaissance at Washington University in St. Louis, though I also studied creative nonfiction under Charles Newman while I was there. I taught a couple of years in Arkansas after that, and I've been teaching at OBU since 2005.

And it's fair to say Oklahoma is a large part of your identity?
Yes, absolutely. The human creation was formed from the dust, and
the dust I was formed from is the dust of Oklahoma. I don't accept
the view of human beings as autonomous individuals. I believe a
person is made up to a great extent by the people and the places that
give the person shape. I try to keep this in mind constantly in my
writing as well as in the choices I make economically and politically.
My wife and I very deliberately chose to move back to the town we
grew up in and root our family there.

**I can certainly relate to that as a native Oklahoman who settled
back closer to home. How have your teaching and writing careers
informed each other?**
Teaching at a small liberal arts college means I get to teach a wide
range of texts and topics, especially in our Western Civ. core classes
and in our great books honors program. This kind of wide reading in
the best that has been written, I hope, keeps my writing grounded in
a tradition and discussion longer, wider, and deeper than the literary
trends of the moment.

**How would you describe your primary values or priorities in your
writing life? I know, for example, that you care deeply about cultivating an authentic sense of place—in other words, taking an
incarnational approach—which shows up both in your own poetry
and in your recent book, *A Poetics of Orthodoxy*.**
Yes, I think "incarnational" covers it well. I believe poetry should be
grounded in observation and in the physical world. We are embodied
beings, and all our experiences are, in some way, embodied experiences.
I don't think abstractions have the power to really move us: emotion
needs physical context. Poetry needs concrete imagery for the same
reason true affection needs the embrace.

How have you seen these values evolve in your own writing? I'm thinking of, for example, the eclectic work in your first collection, *Elegy for Trains*, compared to your more ambitious sonnet sequence, *Black Sunday*: each informed by your Oklahoma heritage but taking distinct forms.

Well, I think my commitment to the concrete and embodied has stayed fairly consistent. What has changed is that I have become a more and more committed "formalist." I rarely write free verse these days, though I often work in a fairly loose blank verse. I admire a lot of free verse poets still, but I find I need the tightness of the metrical line to give measure and balance to the melody of sound. I also prefer to speak within the longer metrical tradition. Free verse in its original moment got a lot of energy out of the act of smashing the dominant English iamb, but I think that energy is quickly waning. Free verse is a reactionary structure, and eventually it becomes self-cannibalizing, endlessly deconstructing itself into smaller bits and more "white space" on the page. Or it lapses into chopped-up prose. The art of meter offers, I think, not only more staying power but also more pleasure for the reader.

That art has stood out to me recently as I've been diving into the work of a shared favorite of ours (and fellow Oklahoma poet), John Berryman—someone who often remained loyal to the iambic line despite his various poetic innovations. What made you decide to turn these observations into a book of criticism? How would you describe reactions to your poetic philosophy? I know you sometimes face resistance from people who think it's too judgmental to declare certain poems as objectively "bad."

Yup, I get a fair bit of "how dare you?!" But I felt like the suggestions and principles in the book would actually be useful to someone who wanted to improve his or her art. The book is based very much on what I have taught in my creative writing classes at OBU for the last fifteen years or so, and I have seen students again and again drastically improve over the course of a semester or two. So I thought the book might be useful, not just to people who want to write poetry, but also to anyone who might want to read poems or to think about how aesthetic standards might be grounded in theological principles. But if one is thoroughly committed to a bland equality in all things artistic, then this is probably a book to take a pass on.

Are there any major criteria that contemporary poets can generally agree upon for evaluating a poem? In other words, is there still a consensus around certain standards of craft despite the wide-ranging shifts that have occurred in American poetry over the past century?

I'd really like to say there are still widely agreed-upon standards, but I would be very hard pressed to say what they are. So I think I'd have to say that American poetry is in a state of nearly total aesthetic anarchy. There is a tendency to decry any suggestion of universal standards, coupled with a tendency to turn around and treat the merest whims of fashion or personal preference as if they carried the weight of a universal standard. I'd say that the lack of wider agreement leads to a sort of tyranny of the trendy.

I understand what you mean, but I will say I see a lot of heated debates about line breaks, at least. What do you see as the major challenges in teaching creative writing to students today? What would you like to see more of in your students' poetry?

I'd say that the lack of shared aesthetic standards we were just talking about is one of the major challenges. A lot of students come in with the notion that the whole of art is simply to say how they feel. Of course, the best cure for that is wide and deep reading in poetry, in the best poetry. I have an advantage in this in teaching in an institution with a strong core curriculum that has them read biblical poetry, Homer, the great Romantics, and so much more. Immersion in the poetic tradition gives a student the right kind of ambition for his or her work and should help to clear away the tendency to be too easily satisfied with one's own efforts. A poet should want to read everything.

What approaches to teaching creative writing have you found particularly effective?
I have nothing against the workshop method, when the most experienced poet in the room (the professor, one assumes) is fully involved in the workshop conversation. I think, however, that the workshop needs to be balanced with days of more formal instruction: craft talks, lectures in the history of poetics, close readings of good examples, etc. I will usually balance a class that meets Tuesdays and Thursdays, for instance, by doing more formal learning one day and workshop the other. Of course, I believe in giving a lot of good reading assignments. If beginning (or intermediate or advanced) poets are reading only the work of their peers, that is bound to be a disaster.

Speaking for myself as a former student of yours, I can say that building a commitment to embodying a physical space in poetry has strengthened my own writing in many ways. By focusing on concrete images and letting them speak for themselves, I've often been surprised by the deeper sacramental meanings that can emerge within the space of a particular poem as I'm in the drafting process. Do you think this is a unique feature to poetry—or at least poetic approaches to language? I'm sure we could both list off plenty of similar examples in well-written novels or other creative genres. But what makes a poem special in this respect?
I think you are right to describe it as a feature of "poetic approaches

to language." To put that another way, the sacramental element in poetry comes from the attempt to bridge the gap between world and word, which can happen in prose too. Other arts work with embodiment in different ways: dance through the movement of the body, painting through the texturing of the paint, music through rhythm. That's why, by the way, I think abstract painting can be sacramental in a way that abstract poetry cannot; the painting has physicality built in, while the poem needs to strive the other way, against abstraction. So I think the goal of incarnation is the same in every art form but that poetry's relationship to embodiment is unique because the means matter.

So why do we see so many poems hovering in a disembodied abstract or philosophical space? Is this approach always ill suited to poetry, or are there good examples of this strategy?
Well, honestly, I think one root cause of abstraction in poetry is just laziness. Observation of the physical world takes effort at attention. I think many poets also simply mistake what makes a poem powerful. They think using emotional words will result in emotion in the reader. But abstractions don't move us. "I'm sad because we're in exile" does nothing to me, but "By the waters of Babylon, we sat down and wept" puts me in the place where the emotion is felt.

I, of course, don't mean that there is no place for abstraction. A lot depends on the length of the poem. A haiku has no room for anything but the primary thing: direct observation of concrete reality. *Notes Toward a Supreme Fiction* or *The Four Quartets*, because so much longer, can afford a little more abstraction, though I might hazard to say that both have a little too much of the abstract still. Very simply, the longer the poem the more abstraction can be sprinkled in, but the grounding in the concrete always has to take precedence.

Are there any poetic images that you think should be off limits for being too cliché? I had another writing teacher once who told me he never wanted to see another bird poem again, for instance. Look, if I tried to make any hard and fast rules here, I would only end up breaking them myself. I don't think the problem is that the images are worn out, but rather that they need to be seen from a new angle. Maybe we get tired of bird poems that show us nothing new, but a poem that makes us see something in the bird that we haven't seen before—well, that's something worth trying for.

How can poets resist temptations toward the abstract or cliché? I think it takes effort and willingness to write slowly, by which I mean a willingness to take seriously "revision" as the poem process. It might help to think more about "building" poems than about writing them, since "writing" suggests something more linear than composition perhaps should be. It also helps if you learn to trust your reader. Abstraction and cliché are very often the result of being afraid that your reader will miss something if you don't spell it out or make it glaringly familiar. Trust your reader and you can write better work.

Who are some poets we should be reading as strong examples of incarnational poetry? One of my favorite things about your poetic philosophy is how you appreciate writers across the formal spectrum. Yeats and Frost are my great inspiration on that. Even at his most immersed state in a very abstract system of belief, Yeats is wedded to the concrete symbol. Frost is the master American poet of place. Jane Kenyon is superb in conveying feeling through image, in restrained and melodic free verse. I think Kenyon was one of the greatest poets of her generation. Elizabeth Bishop is wonderful at capturing the concrete image in language that reinforces it; I'm thinking particularly of "The Fish" but also "The Moose" and many more. I always recommend the Tang dynasty Chinese poets for this, especially Du Fu. Among our contemporaries, I would steer people to Andrew Hudgins, A.E. Stallings, and Joe Weil, for starters.

What kind of work are you up to these days? You have a new collection coming out next year?

Teaching and family life keeps me pretty busy, but I have some essays in the works on education and the liberal arts. I'm working on the finishing touches for a manuscript of poems that should be out soon.[1] I'm still a little obsessed with sonnets.

---

1. *The Family Book of Martyrs* was published by Lamar University Literary Press in 2022.

Acknowledgments

I am grateful to the editors and readers of the journals, magazines, and websites below, where many of these essays and reviews have appeared before. I have often altered these pieces slightly, usually to adjust for the passing of time but also occasionally to correct my own stupidity. Some of the titles are different from that the piece first appeared under. I have not, however, altered at all the thrust of the argument or the line of inquiry.

32 Poems (online):
    "Alfred Corn" (2014)
The American Conservative (online):
    "How the Liberal Arts College Can Save Civilization" (2020)
    "How the Small Liberal Arts College Can Thrive" (2021)
Books and Culture:
    "Paul Mariani" (2014)
Christianity and Literature:
    "Geoffrey Hill" (2015)
Connotation Press:
    "Charles Bernstein" (2011)
Crosstimbers Magazine:
    "Leviathan and the Covenant of Local Commerce" (2010)

First Things (online):
"The Fraud of Higher Education" (2019)
Front Porch Republic:
"Ambiguity and Belonging in Oklahoma" (2023)
"Tradition and Convention" (2023)
"I'm Over the American Homer" (2021)
The Gospel Coalition:
"A Disgusting Poem about God's Goodness" (2020)
The Imaginative Conservative:
"The Christian University: Steward of Western Civilization" (2017)
"Poetry in the Age of Superficiality" (2018)
"Six Poets for People Who Think They Hate Poetry"
(as "Six Poets to Make You Fall for Poetry") first appeared in the
Spring/Summer 2017 POETRY issue of *Oklahoma Humanities*
magazine. Used by permission of *Oklahoma Humanities*, publisher.
"Hunting Berryman's Ghost in Oklahoma" appeared in the February
2018 issue of *Oklahoma Today*.
Ruminate:
"Jeanne Murray Walker" (2016)
Whale Road Review:
"Form from Dust" (2023)
World Literature Today:
"Mary Oliver" (2013)
"C. K. Williams" (2016)

A former poet laureate of Oklahoma, Benjamin P. Myers is the author of four books of poetry and one previous book of nonfiction. His poems, essays, and stories have appeared in *Image*, *First Things*, *Rattle*, *The Yale Review*, and many other places. At Oklahoma Baptist University, Myers directs the Great Books honors program and is the Crouch-Mathis Professor of Literature. He is a contributing editor for *Front Porch Republic* and writes from Chandler, Oklahoma.

Belle Point Press is a literary small press
along the Arkansas-Oklahoma border.
Our mission is simple: Stick around and read.
Learn more at bellepointpress.com.

BELLE
POINT
PRESS